Marcie Stuchin   Susan Abramson

WATERSIDE HOMES

Foreword by
Katherine Pearson
Vice President & Editor

COASTAL
LIVING

PBC INTERNATIONAL, INC.

Distributor to the book trade in the United States and Canada
Rizzoli International Publications, Inc.
through St. Martin's Press
175 Fifth Avenue
New York, NY 10010

Distributor to the art trade in the United States and Canada
PBC International, Inc.
One School Street
Glen Cove, NY 11542

Distributor throughout the rest of the world
Hearst Books International
1350 Avenue of the Americas
New York, NY 10019

Library of Congress Cataloging-in-Publication Data
Stuchin, Marcie.
    Waterside Homes / by Marcie Stuchin and Susan Abramson.
       p.   cm.
    Includes index.
    ISBN 0-86636-631-8 (hardcover). — ISBN 0-86636-632-6 (pbk.)
    1. Seaside Architecture. 2. Architecture, Domestic.
3. Architecture, Modern — 20th century. I. Abramson, Susan.
II. Title.
NA7574.S78 1998
728—dc21   98-37057
                                                           CIP

CAVEAT—Information in this text is believed accurate, and will pose
no problem for the student or casual reader. However, the authors
were often constrained by information contained in signed release
forms, information that could have been in error or not included
at all. Any misinformation (or lack of information) is the result of
failure in these attestations. The authors have done whatever is
possible to insure accuracy.

10 9 8 7 6 5 4 3 2 1

Printed in Hong Kong

For Mallory,
    Whose intelligence and contagious
enthusiasm supported me in every phase
of this project.

                                    M.S.

To Steve, with love—
    Surely all this is not without meaning.

                                    S.A.

contents

foreword

foreword

Many poets have tried to capture the romance, rhythm and timeless continuity of great bodies of water. In a speech to the America's Cup crews, John Fitzgerald Kennedy's explanation was elemental: " ...all of us have in our veins the exact same percentage of salt in our blood that exists in the ocean.... We are tied to the ocean. And when we go back to the sea—whether it is to sail or to watch it—we are going back from whence we came."

Whatever that intangible quality may be, there is no argument that the water pulls on all of us. *Waterside Homes* showcases dwellings around the world, built where they are because of the water and designed to make the most of the water around them, whether ocean, lake, or river. Though water enhances each

of these houses, the ideas within *Waterside Homes* transcend location, as comfortable spaces, casual decorating, and rugged materials are enduring criteria for good design.

Though diverse in style and geography, these homes share common traits. Orientation to the water guides the siting and design of these homes, and the photographs chronicle some of the world's most enviable vistas. Not surprisingly, walls of glass and open floor plans distinguish these homes and dramatize the light and views. Materials respond to the tough climate one contends with as a trade-off for living on the water—humidity, salt water, sand, and wind. Stylishly furnished porches extend the living spaces into the great outdoors, and almost without exception, each house features

one restful, intimate room that functions as a hideaway from the big, open spaces planned for family living.

The decorating styles emphasize comfort and speak as much to the times we live in as to shoreline proximity. The houses here reflect a diversity of life styles. Certainly the more our lives and schedules are filled with work, commitment to family time, fitness, and active volunteerism, the more our homes must be flexible and adapt to change.

Whether you can hear a river rushing over rocks, waves breaking on the beach, or simply the quietness of a still lake, water generates peace, and the interiors within this book reflect that serenity. Yet this is not minimalism. These homes are rich with well-loved objects and furnishings that carry stories with them, without a restricting formality.

Time may prove, in fact, that authors Marcie Stuchin and Susan Abramson are documenting a vital new design movement. At their very best, our homes are a reflection of our life styles. And the design elements in *Waterside Homes* embody the direction we are moving—toward a more connected life. I'm sure the owners would tell you that their homes on the water are much more than scenic retreats, that the houses have become for them a new way to approach their lives.

Katherine Pearson
Vice President and Editor
Coastal Living

introduction

introduction

Who wouldn't want to live by the water? Few of us have ever walked barefoot on a white sandy beach, paddled a canoe on a pristine lake, or viewed a setting sun as it slowly sinks into the ocean without fantasizing about someday finding an equally picturesque site on which to build the house of our dreams.

Waterside Homes...the very phrase evokes images of tranquillity, spirituality, timelessness, and renewal. Water speaks its own language—the hypnotic sound of waves gently breaking on a shore, the empowered roar of a fierce stormy sea. Homes with water views promote a relaxed way of life, one that is less structured and lighter in spirit. Their rooms are filled with fond reflections of the endless summers of youth, and the free-spirited ambience that results when boundaries between indoors and outdoors disappear.

No longer strictly relegated to summer vacations, waterside homes provide an opportunity to capture the spirit of summer living all year. The variety of locations included in our tour of *Waterside Homes* illustrates the diversity of design and decoration prevalent today. We have discovered innovative examples all over the world, from modest bungalows to majestic villas, from classic shingle-style cottages to modernist statements of concrete, steel, and glass.

For the design professional, the waterside home presents a multitude of new freedoms, mandates, and challenges. Maximization of the site is imperative—the home must be sensitive to its setting, whether

it is perched on a cliff overlooking San Francisco Bay or on a preserved wetland in the Hamptons. Unobstructed views of the water are essential. Placement of windows, transparent walls, and open terraces are crucial elements in a home where beautiful vistas are the primary focus.

Most often, waterside designs are dictated by the clients' requests. In many of the homes that follow, informality and ease of care were prerequisites. A Boston entrepreneur envisioned a home on Martha's Vineyard that was "barrier free." One couple desired a home constructed only from natural materials which would blend with the marshland environment. Alternatively, some clients prefer a more elegant waterside aesthetic. Like their more casual counterparts, these homes vary in use and scale, but all are fully equipped with luxurious amenities and gracious detail.

Weather can be both friend and foe to the professional who designs a waterside home. A pavilion in the tropics should offer both sunny and shady spots, and also provide ventilation to capture cool breezes. In areas where hurricanes and severe storms are perennial threats, protection from driving horizontal rain, floods, and beach erosion are critical considerations. All must be dealt with artfully and efficiently in order for the total design to work.

The 37 inspired homes in this volume prove that there is no single formula that works for every design. Each home is uniquely influenced by the designer's response to its surroundings and the personal styles of the people who have chosen to live there. What they all have in common is an ineffable passion for the magic and allure of a water view.

Marcie Stuchin & Susan Abramson

architecturally
speaking

maritime modern

The northern beaches of Australia, with vast golden shores, are a favorite among champion surfers and considered one of the world's most beautiful coastlines. Here, in an established peninsula community, highly desirable because of its 20-kilometer commute to downtown Sydney, a professional couple chose to build their dream house. The design for the site, a steep rise which enjoys staggering unrestricted views of the ocean, was entrusted to Mark Jackson of JACKSON POOLE RABINOWITZ, an award winning Sydney based architectural firm.

The house, which sits proudly perched over the beach, was naturally inspired by its maritime environment. Ship-like curves are found in the undulating lines of its balconies and roofs. A pointed bowsprit balcony thrusts toward the ocean like the head of a ship. The view is of paramount importance and therefore, the architects made generous use of glass walls in all major living areas. Numerous skylights are strategically placed but treated with temperate control film, offering an abundance of natural light while providing shelter from the searing midday Australian sun. No air conditioning was used, only natural ventilation.

Because of the sloping site, the residence is supported on bored pier footings in single and cluster pier groups, which transfer all loads to the underlying rock strata.

photographer: ERIC SIERINS
design budget: $1,100,000
square feet/meters: 6,459/600

center The home is perched on bored pier footings both for structural support and to maximize the view. **above** The narrow front of the house belies its wide sloping exterior. **left** The forward deck, with its rounded balcony, echoes the bow of a ship. A translucent glass wall protects against high winds.

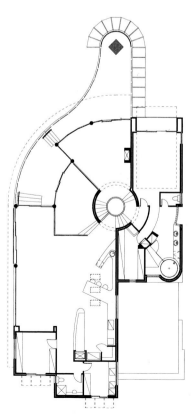

opposite left The architects describe the roofs as shell-like forms. The gradual widening of the house is seen from street to ocean. **opposite right** The central staircase was inspired by the winding formation of those seen in lighthouses. **above** The interior was kept mostly loft-like. Only natural materials were used including timber flooring, wicker furniture and cotton fabrics. **left** Glass walls allow views of the ocean from major living areas, including the kitchen.

cliffdwellers

It was the majesty of the bay view, encompassing the skylines of San Francisco, Berkeley, Oakland and Richmond, that captured the imagination of Angela Danadjieva of DANADJIEVA & KOENIG ASSOCIATES, ARCHITECTS. Anxious to design her residence near San Francisco, Danadjieva chose Tiburon. Her dream site, considered unbuildable by local developers, was perched on the lip of a steeply sloping hillside. Undaunted by the precarious terrain, Danadjieva designed a structure secured by 20-foot deep support piers which descended to the bedrock below. The house was purposely designed with a small foundation footprint to keep down the number of costly piers and preserve the integrity of the natural rock formations and wooded surroundings.

The goal was to create a structure that would blend harmoniously with the bay and hillside topography. They did so with a clever visual mitigation device by cantilevering the living space—living room, dining room, guest room and kitchen—over the middle and lower floors. The structural base houses the architectural studio while the middle floor provides three more bedrooms, a kitchenette and a den. Heavy timber was employed for the 10' x 12' posts and beams supporting the residence, echoing the home's wooded

surroundings. The rich patina of natural wood enhances both interior and exterior settings. Even the landscape design was intended to blend with the topography. Indigenous stones were used for retaining walls that extend the hill's natural rocky character.

photographer: © J.F. HOUSEL
design budget: NOT DISCLOSED
square feet/meters: 3,500/325

center & left Perched on the lip of the hillside, architect Angela Danadjieva's house has won national and international acclaim for its imaginative design, one that blends harmoniously with its surroundings. Cantilevered levels seemingly float above the structural base providing the residents with immediate impact of the view of San Francisco Bay. **above** The deck off the upper floor, which functions as the public living space, displays an African table and stools. The unobstructed view of the bay showcases Angel Island and Kiel Cove.

opposite & above The highlight of the home is the dramatic living room, with its intricately woven ceiling of Douglas fir inspired by tree branches in the neighboring forest. The tightly woven radial-rafter system is centered around a compression ring. Concealed lighting outlines the ceiling shapes and wall panels. **left** The heavy timber beams and rough-sawn pine which characterize the home are evident in this second-floor bedroom.

getting it bright

Florida architect Carey McWhorter of McWHORTER ARCHITECTS is a modernist who knows all about living on the Gulf Coast. Oceanfront homes in the nearby town of Grayton Beach can be subject to destructive tides, storm-eroded dunes, and hurricane force winds of up to 200 miles per hour. The challenge was to create a spirited weekend house that made optimum use of its site while also providing safety from nature's fury.

With no building restrictions to adhere to, the architect launched the design plan by angling the house on its 100' X 100' site, orienting it toward the setting sun and rolling dunes, and designing a bridge-like structure to raise the living areas and bedrooms one story above the sand. Because it is supported by poured-concrete pilings rather than wood, the number of pilings required was reduced—and the view of the adjacent nature preserve enhanced.

On three sides of the lofty 40-foot-long great room soaring windows flood the interior with light. Spare furnishings in bright popsicle tones define the sun-drenched living-dining area, and the grape colored stucco fireplace wall enhances the total composition with bold forms and materials.

photographer: GARY CLARK AS SEEN IN *COASTAL LIVING*
design budget: $550,000
square feet/meters: 4,800/446

center The home has a commanding presence overlooking the dunes. Two deck levels extend the interior space and provide expansive views of the beach and beyond. **above** Both upper and lower decks run the full length of the 40-foot great room. The natural color of the floor provides a warm counterpoint to the white deck chairs and trim. **left** From the ground level a stairway leads to the deck.

opposite To withstand high winds, the expanse of glass windows is reinforced with steel dividers. Small hopper windows, which tilt open for cross-ventilation, line up beneath larger fixed windows. The clerestory windows offer a glimpse of the upper deck. **above left** Since they have three young children, the owners requested a low maintenance home. Throughout the great room oak floors are painted gray. **above** Strong warm colors look vibrant in the sun washed great room. A bold stucco fireplace wall saturated with grape-soaked lyme-based paint complements pillow-like sectional seating. **left** Dormitory-style bunk beds add a delightful dimension to the children's huge ground level playroom. For easy maintenance, sand can be swept from the concrete floor directly onto the driveway.

compound views

A vacation home on Cape Cod needed to serve multiple purposes for a professional couple with grown children. So the couple hired William L. Kite, Jr. of WILLIAM L. KITE ARCHITECTS who designed a flexible family compound that meets their myriad needs, whether hosting formal dinner parties, housing weekend guests, or enjoying a secluded getaway.

Kite planned a structure that is at once contemporary and compatible with Cape Cod's indigenous architectural traditions. Simple in design yet modern in character, the house combines the silvered cedar shingles, dormers and gable roofs of classic New England seaside homes with a generous expanse of windows allowing for ocean views from every major room. Designed to blend harmoniously with its environment, the plan of the compound is composed of elementary sculptural and architectural forms.

The home, a series of four distinct pitched roof buildings arranged informally and linked by single-story, flat-roofed transparent connectors, enjoys different angles of the magnificent view from each component. The first floor of the main house contains the informal sitting area, kitchen, and dining room. Guest rooms are on the second floor. On the

other side of the main house, a one-story structure houses the gracious double height living room. Within its wedge-shaped connector to the main house is a large space used as a formal dining area that accommodates twelve. Behind the central component is the master bedroom and freestanding octagonal master bath. Another two-story structure positioned closest to the entry road contains a garage below and caretaker quarters above.

photographer: ©AARON USHER III
design budget: NOT DISCLOSED
square feet/meters: 4,500/418

center & above Vernacular building forms were used for the main building elements. The roof and wall shingles clad in cedar have weathered to a silvered seaside patina, while mahogany windows, doors, and exposed trim have been stained a transparent red. **left** The angled forms of this Cape Cod vacation house allow for a variety of outdoor areas. Open terraces, accessible to all major living spaces, allow for sunny and shady spots.

opposite The living room's grand scale is enhanced by the imposing fieldstone hearth and anchored by Scarborough Philips' generously scaled furnishings. Exposed wood roof framing and trusses have been painted white to match the walls and ceiling. **above** Stained mahogany trim and custom cabinets highlight the informal dining room and sitting area. **left** The formal dining room is an airy wedge-shaped connector between the double height living room and the main house. Painted steel trusses reinforce the beams. A glass dining table, which easily accommodates twelve, echoes the transparency of the connectors.

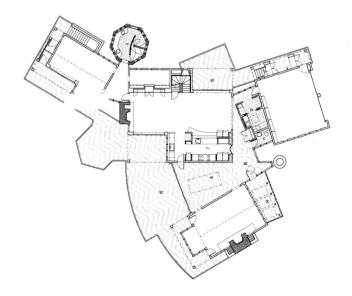

modernist palazzo

The oceanfront walk of Venice is a prized location in this diverse urban beach town. Steven Ehrlich of STEVEN EHRLICH ARCHITECTS, well known for his modernist approach to forms and spaces, took full advantage of a narrow lot when he designed an elongated beach cottage to "grow" from its site. Striping the precast concrete masonry structure with bands of terra-cotta brick, he paid tribute to the Italian architecture for which the town was named.

The home is sandwiched between adjacent houses, yet contains only minimal tall narrow windows on the side walls. Instead, a skylight illuminates the mid-structure of the house where concrete masonry dramatically highlights the entrance. Built on a pedestal that grows into the rooftop sun porch, the house eliminates the boundaries between indoors and out through a repetition of materials expressed in their raw and natural states, and the generous use of glass.

Furnishings throughout are sculptural and modern, further accentuating the simple yet bold composition. Concrete block and structural clay block contrast with the cool slate flooring and add warmth and texture to the beach cottage.

photographer: TOM BONNER 1990
design budget: NOT DISCLOSED
square feet/meters: 3,300/307

center A rooftop crowns the structure, offering the owners and their guests unlimited sun and views of the beach. **above** The design possesses only token fenestration in the side walls. Rich natural grains of the table warm the dining area. **left** A gray concrete block pedestal, striped with terra-cotta brick structural units, raises the lower sun porch above the level of the busy ocean-walk promenade, providing the requisite privacy for the owners.

opposite Geometric metal French doors seem to vanish when open, revealing an ocean view framed by built-in precast masonry units. The fireplace is made from precast concrete. **above left** There is plenty of storage in the sleek compact kitchen. Granite countertops and stainless steel fixtures are striking against white, and echo the colors of the brick stripes and slate floors. **above right** Indoors blends with outdoors—a trademark Ehrlich feature. **left** Terra-cotta banding in the concrete pays tribute to Italian architecture.

lakeside geometry

When looking for a weekend retreat to unwind, a professional couple from Mexico City wanted something practical, informal and elegant. Their children, three boys who are competitive sailors and water-skiers, hoped for a place in a waterside community with tennis facilities as well as a marina for sailing and motorboats. Valle de Bravo, about a two-hour drive from their home in Mexico City, proved to be the perfect year-round resort town. The old village resides around a large lake which is actually a reservoir that supplies water to Mexico City. On its shores, the established family-friendly waterside community partakes in all water sports.

For their family vacation home the clients turned to Mexico's internationally renowned Ricardo Legorreta of LEGORRETA ARQUITECTOS whose work they had often admired, especially the Hotel Camino Real in Ixtapa. Legorreta initiated a plan similar to that of the Ixtapa hotel which adapted to its sloping terrain and provided spectacular views of the lake. Here, on a more intimate scale, elegance, simplicity and local vernacular architecture served as his inspiration. In true Legorreta style he selected only a few simple construction materials: hand-troweled stucco walls, local tile, wooden beams and concrete flooring. Spaces are clear and kept

mostly bare except for necessary furniture. There are no moldings and decorative clichés in Legorreta's work; attention is drawn by the monochromatic use of the color mustard, changing patterns of light, and the magnificent harbor view.

photographer: LOURDES LEGORRETA
design budget: $250,000
square feet/meters: 4,198/390

center The design of the home was planned according to its steep site. Legorreta was requested to build on a small scale so the home naturally rests on a number of different levels. Sloping roofs provide a solution for the terrain and rain. **above** Legorreta utilized color to draw attention to the view. Clean, geometric forms serve as a backdrop for changing light patterns. **left** The house inhabits a steep slope about midway up the hill, affording spectacular views of the Valle de Bravo lake/reservoir.

above The magnificent vista of Valle de Bravo's lake is captured by the simple architecture of the sunken pool. **right** The slate veranda extends to the circular pool. The slope of the roof is echoed in the sloping wall beside it. **opposite (above left)** Ochre walls register patterns of changing light. **opposite (above right)** All bedrooms are furnished simply with bare necessities. The staircase is a geometric design element which leads nowhere. **opposite below** Abundant light pours into the master bedroom from two walls of windows framing the lake view. Simple wooden beamed ceilings are used throughout the home.

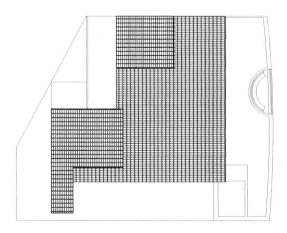

picture perfect

When two young movie moguls wanted to produce one of their most important projects to date—their own residence atop the crest of Pacific Palisades—they hired internationally renowned GWATHMEY SIEGEL & ASSOCIATES to create it for them. The architect's biggest challenge was literally to re-stage the setting—a cliff with barely more than a quarter acre of developable land.

Stabilizing the cliff with 60 caissons sunk 60 feet into the bedrock, and creating a number of retaining walls, the architect produced an elaborate pedestal for a 15,000-square-foot house perched near the top of Malibu Canyon. A three-story curved limestone pavilion constitutes the main living space and faces the Pacific Ocean and the Los Angeles skyline. Behind its sculptural limestone facade is the master bedroom, kitchen, living room, dining room, billiard room and den. Embedded in the slope behind is a three-story cube which stabilizes the residence. The couple uses this space for their offices, conference room, screening room, archives and library. Additionally, there is a large exercise room, guest rooms, children's suite and extensive storage areas.

The Pacific Palisades home is intended to be seen as a series of fragments, evoking a cubist bas-relief. The unique

juxtaposition of shapes—the multilevel curved pavilion, and the three-story cubed support building—forms an abstract collage that endows the house with monumental architectural drama.

photographer: ASSASSI PRODUCTIONS 1997
design budget: NOT DISCLOSED
square feet/meters: 15,000/1,394

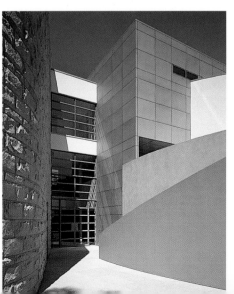

center above The residence is stabilized atop the crest of Pacific Palisades. **center below** An exterior view displays the layout of the main living pavilion fronted by the curved limestone wall. **above** Steel is used as a major architectural element both in the grid of the windows and the staircase railing. The view is of the Malibu Canyon and Will Rogers State Park. **left** The eastern terrace entry displays a collage of materials —cleft-cut limestone blocks, zinc panels, and stucco.

opposite & above left The living room is part of the curved limestone pavilion which faces the Pacific Ocean and the Los Angeles skyline. The sofa and armchairs by Jean-Michael Frank and the Eileen Gray rug are from Ecart International. Charles Gwathmey designed the sofa table, side tables and coffee table. The rocking chair is by Joseph Hoffman. **above** The dining area projects the quiet serenity of an art gallery, with minimalist furnishings and an early-20th-century painting. **left** The screening room is ensconced in the cubed structural support building which also houses his and her offices, and a conference room. The Eames lounge chairs and ottomans are from Herman Miller.

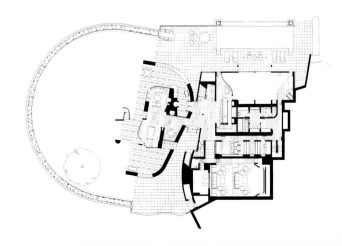

harbor whites

For the Sydney, Australia yachting set, Point Piper is *the* suburban address in which to live. It is situated in one of the exclusive harbor suburbs, an elite strip of waterfront mansions designed by internationally known architects. No wonder a yachting family of four chose this hillside harbor front site, with a deep water mooring, for their primary residence, and entrusted Dennis Rabinowitz of JACKSON POOLE RABINOWITZ ARCHITECTS and Robert Grubb of ROBERT GRUBB & ASSOCIATES to design it for them.

The owners dreamed of a home that would re-create the whitewash of Greek island villas and the open-sided architecture of the South Pacific. The architect envisioned the house as a 'village', a Balinese pavilion-like complex consisting of chief's hut, children's hut, and a central space for cooking, eating and socializing. The completed home, with its minimalist detailing, staggered levels, and myriad views from courtyards and roof terraces, contains an eclectic mix of styles from around the world. Yet, it is completely at home at Sydney Harbor, where many grand turn-of-the-century dwellings have been replaced with newer, more innovative designs.

Rabinowitz and Grubb incorporated a strong interconnection between the interior and exterior design by maintaining a

uniformity of materials and finishes, and using slide-away window walls. Large weather-resistant timber pergolas covered with lush climbing plants shade the northern exposures of the home and further the breezy transition from indoor space to outdoor terraces.

photographer: PATRICK BINGHAM-HALL
design budget: NOT DISCLOSED
square feet/meters: 7,022/653

center & left The wet edge of the pool vanishes gracefully into the harbor. Terraced garden areas were inspired by the landscapes of Ubud, Bali. **above** A prized location ideal for a boating family, the property has a boathouse and a deep water dock.

opposite With its staggered levels, courtyards and roof terraces, this home "down under" obtains views from numerous vantage points and achieves northern sunlight. Its design was conceived as an eclectic mix of New Mexico pueblo, Greek island villa, and Pacific island pavilion. **above left** Sliding glass doors add a pavilion-like ambience to the rustic structure. The blond beech timbers used for the pergolas throw shadows and light onto matte finished walls. **above & left** A commanding stairway is sculpturally exposed. To shield against maritime corrosion, glass balustrades were used throughout the home. Sunlight is diffused through louvred shades.

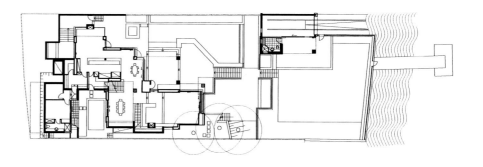

sea glass

Few city dwellers are lucky enough to have ocean beaches within the boundaries of their own metropolis. Rio de Janeiro has Ipanema, Miami has Miami Beach, and Los Angeles has Santa Monica and Venice. But the inherent challenge of a beach-within-a-city is that of limited beachfront living space. In Santa Monica, where narrow building lots are bordered on one side by the Pacific Ocean and on the other by the Pacific Coast Highway, beach properties are highly coveted commodities.

Without sacrificing space or luxury, STEVEN EHRLICH ARCHITECTS and designer MARLO WOLFE squeezed a 16-foot wide home into a narrow slice of land with direct access to the Santa Monica beach and ocean walk. The lofty proportions of this 45-foot tall beach house speak to the creativity of the designers and the young family who lives in it. At once providing privacy and unrestricted views of the ocean, the design employs windows tinted in shades of sea glass on the outside, yet yield a clear view from within. The building materials, structural steel and tinted concrete, shield the home from environmental foes—earthquakes, wind, salt, and highway noise. Cool tones, inside and out, integrate the brilliant blues and greens of the seascape.

photographer: GREY CRAWFORD
design budget: NOT DISCLOSED
square feet/meters: 3,500/325

~~~~~~

center The side elevation shows a modernist use of concrete and glass shaded in colors of the seascape. The lower central panel is a wall of green-tinted glass. **above** The fireplace mantel is stucco pigmented with the color of the sea. **left** The beach facade of the house is marked by a dramatic geometry of shapes and expansive views.

above The main stairway is a composition of shape and form. An opaque grid of Kal-Wall ensures total privacy from next door neighbors. **above right** Laminated glass provides a translucent opalecence to the windows and roll-up doors. **right** "Let's do lunch!"—The owners requested a design for the kitchen that showcases their campy collection of vintage lunch boxes. **opposite** On the top floor, the master bedroom and balcony command the most dramatic views of the beach.

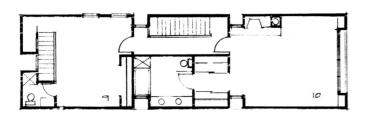

elegant living

pop art & palms

The building designed by Edward Durrell Stone on "Mansion Row" is one of the most attractive apartment buildings in Palm Beach. Having long admired its early sixties' architecture, GEOFFREY N. BRADFIELD chose a duplex apartment there, overlooking a three-mile stretch of beach with unparalleled views of the Atlantic Ocean, for his own weekend getaway.

The central location of the apartment, only one block from Worth Avenue, provides him with a change of venue in which to unwind, swim, and bike. As a satellite office, Bradfield can also use it to design projects in his trademark—a refined, modernist style.

For his personal haven Bradfield aimed for a relaxed and comfortable atmosphere. A model of cool restraint, the real focus of the design is the spectacular view and his powerful collection of contemporary and pop art. Throughout the open plan downstairs and the more private upper level bedrooms and baths, important works from such modern masters as Andy Warhol and Salvador Dalí have turned the entire duplex into a stunning gallery of 20th-century art and design.

photographer: ROBERT BRANTLEY
design budget: NOT DISCLOSED
square feet/meters: 2,000/186

center The supper table is set with Daum's whimsical china and stemware. Two bronze lifeguards by Auroro Camero watch over the beachfront. **above & left** In the living room, sophisticated pop art shares equal billing with primitive Cameroon handcrafted pieces. A Kenneth Nolan oil on canvas is highlighted by the crisply restrained white furnishings. The bronze table sculpture is by Lynn Chadwick.

opposite Warhol's commanding double portrait of Elvis dominates the living room wall. The sculptural French art deco screen, a flea market find, precedes the leopard carpeted staircase. **left** In the master bedroom, Dali's *La Persistance de la Memoire* "marks time." A John Cocteau crayon drawing is artfully placed above a striped, French art moderne chair.

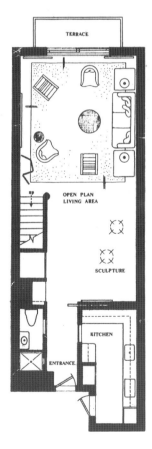

TERRACE

OPEN PLAN
LIVING AREA

SCULPTURE

KITCHEN

ENTRANCE

all about eaves

Picturesque communities dot the New England coastline and in summer, pine forests, cranberry bogs, and roses blanket the landscape. The Atlantic Ocean provides an exquisite backdrop for a waterfront home, but it can also play a villainous role when it comes to the severe weather that Mother Nature occasionally bestows on its shores.

High winds, rain, and coastal flooding were forces to be reckoned with when architect Thomas Nugent of PETER PENNOYER ARCHITECTS designed this grand seaside home. The clients desired a vacation home with maximum views and exposure to the water. The architects incorporated the shingle-style vernacular popularized by turn-of-the-century New England seaside cottages. Sloped roofs and eaves, and porches with deep overhangs were employed to shield against potentially destructive weather.

The shingled simplicity of the exterior is elegantly balanced with the home's gracious interiors. Classical elements of colonial revival architecture—formal moldings and coffered ceilings—help identify the downstairs living areas. To maintain the degree of informality central to a family vacation home, the kitchen, dining area, and living room were kept open, yet each room retains a distinct character.

photographer: © WADE ZIMMERMAN
design budget: NOT DISCLOSED
square feet/meters: 3,600/334

~~~~~~

center The simplicity of the asymmetric structure suggests shingle-style turn-of-the-century seaside homes. **above** The living room's comfortable seating is in the Bridgewater style. The owner's collection of Asian accessories adds color and texture to the warm yet neutral palette. **left** A series of trim, dormered windows look down the sloping site.

opposite French doors and semicircular transoms create luminous interiors and warmth in the living/dining areas. **above left** An open, yet defined dining room provides a social center for the owners and their weekend guests. Meal preparation takes place on the kitchen's center island. **above** A charming bay windowed makeup area extends the bathroom space. Creamy layers of white blend to brighten the view. **left** A Palladian window boasts a dramatic view of the bay. Simple bamboo shades can be drawn for privacy. Through the dormered window the morning sun casts playful shadows on verdant walls.

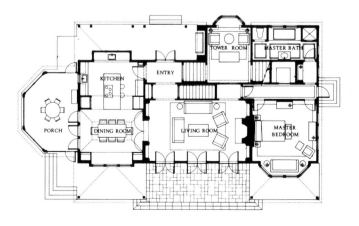

bellavista

Few golf communities on Florida's Intracoastal Waterway boast locations comparable to the Admiral's Cove Yacht and Country Club in Jupiter. The community's golf course is renowned for meticulously groomed fairways and challenging terrain. A clubhouse with tennis courts and a state-of-the-art exercise facility provide a full social schedule.

The most impressive homes in this community look out on the Intracoastal waters. Gregory Gozzo of GOZZO ESTATE HOMES, who builds some of the finest residences in the area, developed a model home here inspired by the grandeur of Italian Mediterranean villas. This property, aptly named "The Positano" incorporates 8,900 square feet of living space. Visitors are immediately dazzled as they pass through the antique hand-finished cypress front door into a rotunda shaped entrance foyer with a 28-foot ceiling. Double height windows in the living room, dining room and family room, flood the space with Florida sunshine. Four immense bedrooms and 6½ baths are situated on the first floor of the villa. A full guest suite is located on the second floor.

When the builders needed someone to set the right tone for the home's interior, they turned to Jack Fhillips of JACK FHILLIPS DESIGN, noted for the elegantly gracious

interiors he created for numerous Mediterranean-inspired residences. Fhillips used only the finest materials and cleverly mixed rare antiques with plush custom upholstery, creating an atmosphere which is quietly breathtaking without ostentation.

photographer: ROBERT BRANTLEY PHOTOGRAPHY
design budget: NOT DISCLOSED
square feet/meters: 8,900/827

center The exterior of "The Positano" is highlighted by its foyer rotunda measuring 28-feet-high with a diameter of 18 feet. Massive stone colonnades support a second-story bridge which wraps around the rotunda. **above** The 8,900-square-foot residence was inspired by Italianate villas. **left** The sunken living room features a fireplace made from hand carved limestone.

opposite Double French doors topped by arched windows provide an infusion of light and warmth in the living room. **above left** In the family room, Fhillips used rich cherry and mahogany furniture to complement the cabinetry in the adjacent kitchen. **above** The stately dining room, like its adjoining living room and foyer, is especially grand due to its soaring ceiling height. A thick marble table is surrounded by wrought-iron chairs. Other high backed chairs are antique Italian. **left** The kitchen features rich cherry cabinetry which Phillips had distressed for an antique finish. An immense stone hearth surrounds the stove top. **following pages** A four poster king-size bed draped with a silk canopy and bedskirt holds center court in the grand master bedroom. Phillips used the finest silk damasks for bed covering and chaise. His choice of terra-cotta color walls underscores the Italian influence seen throughout the residence.

family values

When asked to transform a sprawling turn-of-the-century New England "summer cottage" into a primary residence for an active young family of four, Lee Bierly and Christopher Drake of the Boston-based design team BIERLY-DRAKE ASSOCIATES had their work cut out for them. Since they loved to entertain guests, especially their large extended family, the clients requested a user-friendly design that would be warm and inviting, yet open enough for company to flow freely between parlors, terraces, and the scenic lawns which overlook the Atlantic. In order to accomplish that, walls between some rooms had to be broken down, guest bathrooms were added, and a layout was devised to accommodate the needs of a modern nineties family.

Throughout the shingle-style home, the designers retained its classic architectural integrity, both structurally and decoratively. A sprawling porch and eaves on the water side maximize the expansive views. Furnishings were kept light, imparting a timeless quality to traditional antiques and the owner's extensive collection of Cape Ann art. Original details and fixtures were spared wherever possible. When absent, they were authentically re-created.

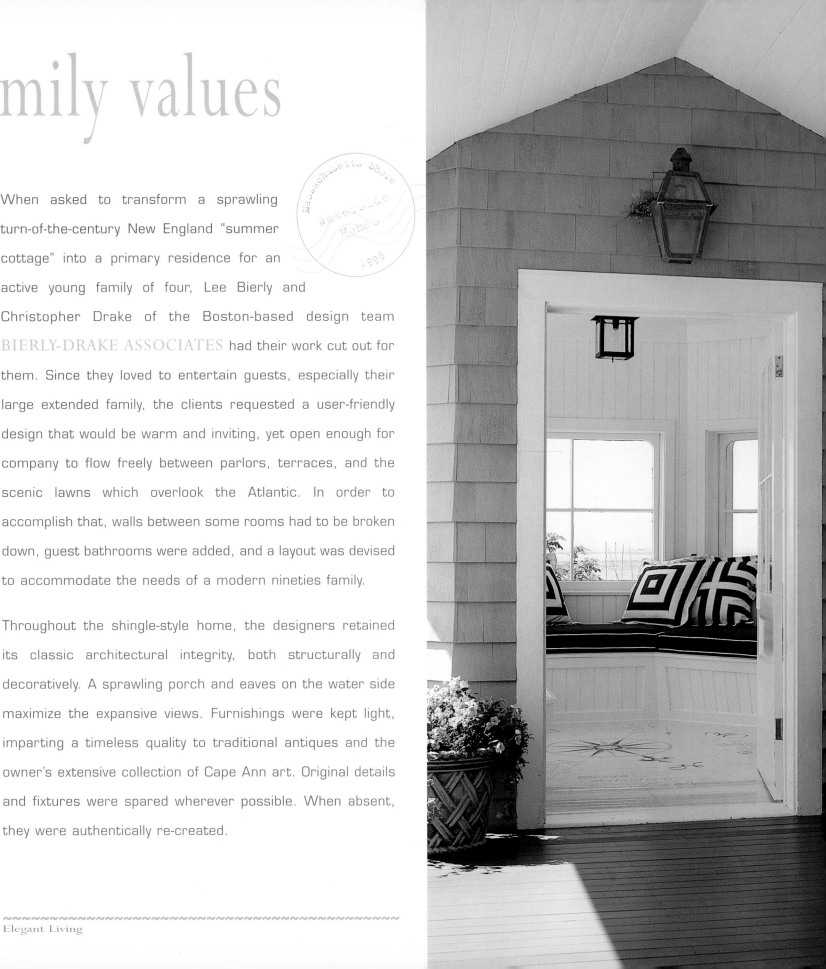

photographer: SAM GRAY
design budget: NOT DISCLOSED
square feet/meters: 8,000/743

center The pilot house, original to the 1907 structure, is an extension of the porch, and looks out to the water. A local artisan painted the compass on the floor to resemble that of an old nautical chart. **above** A white sofa dramatically sets off a contemporary still-life painting in this living area. **left** During the renovation the long porch was widened. Sunbrella fabrics cover the breezy swings and rockers to protect them from the sun and salty air.

above Comfortable seating fills the bay window of the parlor. **right** Beyond the "great hall", a classic traditional dining room is energized by the bright toile wall covering. Two Duncan Fyfe table bases support the extension table that seats twelve. **opposite** Chintz Bridgewater armchairs are poised for private conversation. Period pieces, like the chest-on-chest and gentleman's washstand, are from the early 19th century.

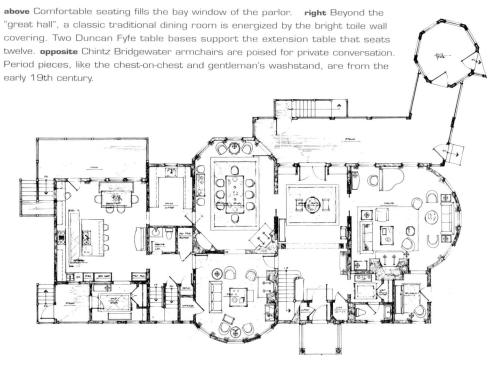

luxe elegance

From concept to christening, the "Indiscretion" was designed to be more than a mere pleasure craft. This magnificent 120-foot yacht is a quintessential floating vacation home defined by modernist style and luxury. It is used to visit ports of call worldwide by its owners— intrepid travelers and collectors who have been members of the international yachting community for decades.

The "Indiscretion" was custom built to perfection by Broward Marine of Florida, superior shipbuilders who skillfully combined state-of-the-art marine technology with old-world craftsmanship. The owner's interior designer, Mitchell J. Rubin of MITCHELL J. RUBIN ASSOCIATES, worked alongside the yacht builders planning all interior spaces and providing architectural details of wood, etched glass, marble, granite, intricate cabinetry and meticulous metalwork.

The clients requested an overall design which was luxurious for entertaining, yet comfortable for family gatherings including grandchildren. For inspiration, the designer was drawn to the great French ocean liners, the *Normandy* and *Ile de France* in which modernist, art deco interiors reflected the essence of gracious style and superior workmanship.

photographer: © WADE ZIMMERMAN
design budget: NOT DISCLOSED
square feet/meters: 120/11

center The main salon displays an inlaid media cabinet wall by Rubin of anigré and sapele woods. **above** The salon features a mirrored cocktail table of the French deco period. Other tables which harmonize with art deco originals were designed by Rubin. **left** The yacht boasts three levels of outside decks for lounging and sunbathing. The second level also accommodates the family car.

opposite The buffet area, located off the main salon, draws its color from an Edward Fields custom carpet based on a thirties French Aubusson by Solnge Patry-Bie. The dining table executed in sapele, polished stainless and glass is based on an original by French maker, Dominique, 1935. Rare candlesticks are by Gio Ponti. **above** Rubin chose rich Clarence House fabrics to upholster the walls and headboard in the master stateroom. The sconces, which are signed by Jules Leleu, circa 1930, complement deco-inspired mahogany cabinetry. **left** The master bath, with its enormous sunken marble tub and rich woodwork only belies its nautical setting because of its porthole window.

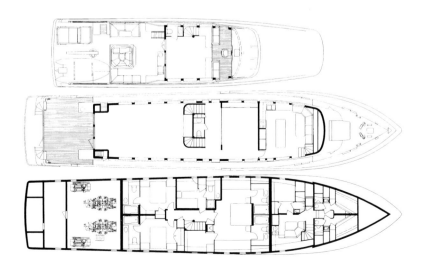

brazilian idyll

Sig Bergamin of SIG BERGAMIN INTERIORS carefully tailors his designs to suit the life styles of his clients. This was the case with a couple from São Paulo who engaged Bergamin to design their vacation home in the prestigious community of Laranjeiras. The land they purchased faces the mountainous countryside, lush with palms and banana trees, and enjoys close proximity to a wide saltwater canal that feeds into the Atlantic Ocean.

The clients requested a hospitable, ample-sized home for their teenage children and year-round family guests. Bergamin created simple unadorned rooms, punctuated with comfortable furniture and colonial period decorative accessories. Windows were expanded in order to adequately capture balmy breezes and profuse natural light. The designer felt the architecture, while essentially contemporary, could capitalize on a Brazilian colonial theme. To this end, he created a great room or living room from which projects a wide veranda. High ceilings, clean architectural lines, simple polished wood floors and a unique mélange of Portuguese, Brazilian and Balinese motifs reflect Bergamin's famously creative skill—inside and out!

photographer: TUCA REINÉS
design budget: $1,000,000
square feet/meters: 11,841/1,100

center The wide veranda off the living room is delightfully cool, enjoying abundant breezes. **above** Balinese chairs on the veranda are covered in blue and white fabric by Ralph Lauren. **left** The sprawling contemporary home, loosely inspired by Brazilian colonial architecture measures 11,841 square feet.

opposite The living room has high ceilings and numerous seating areas to accommodate large family get-togethers and year-round guests. Sofa fabric echoes a tropical motif. Teak wooden furniture reminiscent of the Brazilian colonial period, and natural sisal floor covering create an informal atmosphere. **above left** Bergamin outfitted the dining room with a massive, simple Portuguese table surrounded by chairs bearing a pineapple motif. The large painting depicting Indians showcases the Brazilian historical references found throughout the house. **above** A profusion of white in the kitchen provides a clean backdrop for contemporary facilities. **left** Four poster beds are capped with palm finials. Blue and white cotton fabric displays lush tropical landscapes.

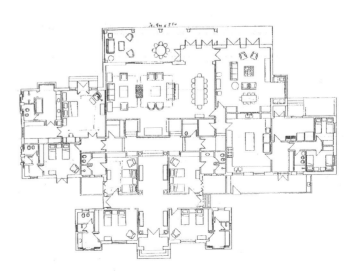

timeless style

Lee Bierly and Christopher Drake of BIERLY-DRAKE ASSOCIATES are noted for their flair for enlivening traditional design with vitality and visual panache. For this reason they were chosen by an active couple with six grown daughters to create a colorful and inviting interior for their spacious vacation home on Cape Cod. Although recently built, the couple wanted their home to project an authentic sense of history.

This is a house for people who enjoy their privacy—the home and its guest cottage are spread out over 20 acres with half a mile of protected private beach. Designed in a typical Bermuda style, the home is set high on the sand dunes above the beach surrounded by marsh grass. Here Bierly and Drake orchestrated a casual floor plan for family living. The effect is light and airy, always emphasizing spectacular sunset views on the outer cape.

To allow for frequent entertaining, Bierly and Drake outfitted three bedrooms in the main house and three in the guest cottage with all the trappings found in casually elegant hotels. Both structures have large flexible entertaining areas. The separate guest house ensures the owner's privacy when visitors linger—it is ten acres away!

photographer: SAM GRAY
design budget: NOT DISCLOSED
square feet/meters: 3,500/325

center The living room of the main house is casually arranged with plump sofas and deep chintz covered chairs. A 19th-century American weathervane and wooden swan are among the many pieces of folk art displayed throughout the house. **above** The family room off the kitchen gets visual punch from the lively graphic design on the wicker chaises and overstuffed cotton sofa with denim pillows. Sliding doors lead to the arbored terrace. **left** A terrace with balcony is accessible off the spacious master bedroom. Simple serenity sets the tone with billowing natural cotton curtains and chaise for lounging or reading.

opposite The dining room is casually elegant. Natural elements including a rope bordered sisal rug, teak dining chairs and simple linen drapes are accented by a whimsical wrought iron etagere and chandelier. **above left** A wall of books and a large wicker chaise serve as the guest house library. Bare wooden plank floors and a painted wooden staircase take the edge off formality. Bare feet are welcome here! **above** The undulating lines of the simple wrought iron bed are echoed in the bedside table lamp. Crisp cotton sheets and wool sisal carpeting are comfortable and cool. **left** The walls of the master bedroom are sponged with a pale pink wash. A simple wrought iron four poster bed is hung with full cotton drapes matching those at the window. A creamy soft wool rug underscores comfort and quiet style.

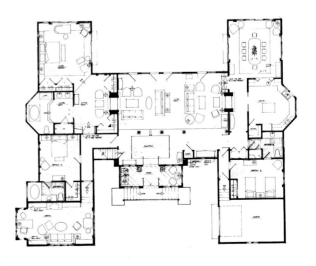

miami rhapsody

The architecture of Miami Beach reflects the cultural influences of its 100-year evolution as a vacation paradise. A legacy of style—from the original Spanish villas of the early century to the streamlined art deco buildings of the thirties and grand hotels of the fifties and sixties, to the Latin bodegas of the seventies and eighties—has been the springboard for a vibrant rebirth of culture and design.

The team of Jean-Pierre Heim and Galal Mahmoud of DESIGN CONNECTION is part of the Miami Beach design explosion. Their colorful blend of Mediterranean styles for a successful young bachelor could easily be at home in Marrakesh or Majorca. Here in Miami Beach it is well suited to the owner's life style. He loves to entertain friends, and an oversized living room that opens to an outdoor terrace provides him with plenty of space for lively catered parties.

Fabrics and furnishings, designed in Paris and shipped to Miami, enhance the total "mood Mediterranean." If there is a dominant theme to the home's interior, it is the varied, vibrant palette. Sun-kissed color, borrowed from homes and buildings of the Riviera, plays against the radiant tones of Miami's sea and sky. The bare terra-cotta floor is a natural anchor to the exuberant wash of color throughout the house.

photographer: GEORGE SHELLEY
design budget: $700,000
square feet/meters: 5,000/465

center Due to the marshy terrain, deep pilings were necessary to build the pool and terrace. Mosaic pool tiles were imported from the south of France. **top** A tile border creates the illusion of an area rug on the terra-cotta floor. Turned pillars accent the grand scale of the room. **above** The home was designed with three comfortable guest rooms, in addition to the owner's bedroom suite, each with its own bath. **left** A cozy daybed, upholstered in faded kilim-patterned linen, is washed with sunlight. An intricately carved altar frames a niche behind it.

peak perfection

Surrounding the noisy, frenetic city of Hong Kong—an international center for finance, trade and manufacturing— are quietly majestic mountain peaks and hundreds of verdant outlying islands. West of the city is the beautiful mountain, Victoria Peak, where luxury apartment buildings and large private houses (rare in Hong Kong) line the steep sides of its slope. Set behind giant private gates in an art deco inspired house with breathtaking views of sky and sea, John Chan of JOHN CHAN DESIGN, one of Hong Kong's most acclaimed hotel and residential interior designers, has created a stunning personal oasis of elegance and tranquillity.

The house formerly belonged to one family and had not been renovated since the thirties. Intent on maintaining the architectural integrity of the classic building, Chan set about reconfiguring the space without making major structural changes. His obvious mandate was to exploit the incredible vista by installing immense wood encased windows.

Chan's desire for spaciousness dictated the floor plan where one room visually flows into the next. A melange of exquisite Chinese and modern furniture and objects are placed sparingly apart. In their spacious arrangement, set off by

warm white walls and cool Italian marble sandstone flooring,

each piece assumes sculptural significance. The overall effect

of the design is a masterful example of East meets West.

photographer: PASCAL BLANCON
design budget: NOT DISCLOSED
square feet/meters: 6,400/595

center The view from the shaded terrace of John Chan's Victoria Peak home is a breathtaking endless vista of sky and sea. Teak furniture and blue and white Chinese garden stools underscore an outdoor elegance. **above** The open balconies and terraces possess different full frontal views of mountain peaks, sea and sky. **left** The main terrace is arranged with teak garden furniture. Railings are made from green bamboo.

opposite Large comfortable rattan furniture surrounds a modern inlaid wood table in the living room where a magnificent view is showcased through double glazed, wood framed windows. Recessed motorized honeycomb shades release to protect the interior from the strong afternoon sun. **left** Donghia chairs and a modern leather sofa are placed beside colonial details in this living area, where high ceilings create a sense of spaciousness. **below left** Pale carpeting, warm wood furnishings and luxurious linens underscore tranquillity in one of the large bedrooms. **below right** Rich woods and art deco mirrors highlight the guest bathroom.

weekend style

An informal waterside retreat in Westport, Connecticut, was the counterbalance to an active city life for an energetic, athletic family with young children. Enlisting interior designer Richard Mervis of RICHARD MERVIS DESIGN, the family embarked on a renovation that developed a conventional eighties contemporary into a casual space, ablaze with tropical color.

Mervis orchestrated the 8,000-square-foot home for stylish family living on winter weekends year-round and for full-time use during the summer. On the first floor is a dramatic double height vestibule and living room. Floor to ceiling windows draw the spectacular view inside. An enormous kitchen, dining room, sunroom, den and master suite are also on this floor. Upstairs are the children's rooms and playroom as well as a guest suite. The selection of colors, fabrics and patterns were chosen from a palette that blends cool hues with warm tones, creating a lively, vivid scheme.

Every room is child-friendly, with comfortable upholstery featuring highly polished durable woods. On the exterior, a putting green is perched on a small hill beside the pool, and a deep water dock is easily accessed for summer recreation.

photographer: PHILLIP ENNIS
design budget: NOT DISCLOSED
square feet/meters: 8,000/743

center Floor to ceiling windows showcase an extraordinary view of Long Island Sound. Mervis selected neutral fabrics for the informal living room. Visual punch is achieved by the colorful art deco-inspired rug and brilliant accent pillows. Rattan chairs are by Bielecky Brothers. The metallic curtain fabric is from Randolf and Hein. **above** Mervis installed a compact but efficient pool house with a wet bar. Stools are from Brown Jordan. **left** A single hole putting green was installed by prior owners, but enjoyed by the current residents.

above Donghia leather chairs surround the walnut dining table. The floors in the living and dining rooms are bleached white oak. **right** Rattan lends a cool blond look to the sunroom. Walls are covered with straw paper from Hinson & Company. **far right** The powder room mirror lends a nautical tone. The walls are enveloped in exotic Indian slate. **opposite** The den was paneled in wood to complement the existing fireplace.

house of windsor

The village of Windsor, near Vero Beach, Florida, has become the new paradigm for community living. Created by the team of Studio Andres Duany and Elizabeth Plater-Zyberk, international leaders in the new return to town planning, Windsor was inspired by such historic towns as St. Augustine, Charleston and Savannah. With its cantilevered balconies and private garden walls, it was designed to conform to architectural guidelines which reinforce the town planning concept of a pedestrian centered outdoor community.

Thomas M. Payette of PAYETTE ASSOCIATES designed a spacious Windsor compound for his family. Payette installed wooden trusses, beams, and plank construction that warm the large, open interior spaces. Twenty-plus-foot-high ceilings in the living room allow for large volumes of air, while the careful placement of windows permits an abundance of sunlight. With two small freestanding buildings for guests in addition to the main house, the entire compound centers around a large outdoor courtyard, with every room opening directly onto it. A continuous flow of activity from the inside rooms to the outside area, effectively erases all boundaries.

photographers: BRIAN VANDEN BRINK & WILLIAM C. MINARICH PHOTOGRAPHY, INC.
design budget: $720,000
square feet/meters: 5,700/530

center Perfect for an evening swim, the pool sparkles from courtyard illumination. **above** To create a harmonious relationship among elements of scale, materials, color and proportion, all buildings of Windsor conform to architectural guide-lines. **left** A trellised walkway, providing shade from the Florida sun, runs the length of the main house.

opposite In the living room, natural light bathes the colorwashed tones of the furniture. Through careful placement of windows and doors, the space captures sunlight throughout the day. **above left** The inside of the home has warm wooden trusses, beams, and plank construction. With its doors wide open, the living room's 20-plus-foot-high ceilings allow for air to circulate by slowly rotating fans. **above** The double height dining room can accommodate formal dinner parties or a casual gathering of grandchildren. **left** Two simple canopied beds are breezily dressed in scrim. Light oak floors and furniture are accented by a colorful throw rug.

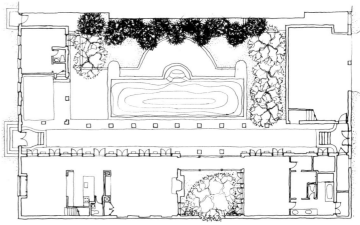

marine life

From their private beach at Angra dos Reis, the owners of this home look out onto an emerald bay. Costa Verde, as the area is appropriately named, is lush

with tropical vegetation and mountainous terrain that hugs the shore of the island-cluttered bays. For a family that loves the sea and the nautical life style it provides, this was the ideal site for a vacation home.

Marco Aurelio Keller Menegazzo of STUDIO MARCO AURELIO MENEGAZZO designed the house with elements from traditional Caribbean architecture. Its two-story structure supports a roof with deep overhangs to provide shade from the tropical sun. In typical Brazilian style, the rooms on both levels open to shaded verandas which face the bay and function as additional living space. From the interior, the focal point of the design is a double-story grid of glass that looks out to the verdant flora.

The interiors incorporate English colonial with indigenous Brazilian styles. Throughout the house the designer used nautical accessories to enhance the furnishings. From antique maritime paintings, to model ships, to decorative boating flags, this home is a testament to the owners' love of the sea.

photographer: TUCA REINÉS
design budget: $2,000,000
square feet/meters: 14,000/1,300

center The two-story home was designed in the Caribbean style, with deep roof overhangs that shelter numerous verandas from the sun. The site offers access to boating and diving from the home's deep water dock. **above** The owner's passion for boating is exemplified by the spacious and inviting living room. Pillows take the form of nautical flags, lending a whimsical touch to comfortable seating. **left** Bright splashes of marine blue upholstery echo the tones of the nearby water.

opposite Sunlight streams through grids of double height windows illuminating a stairway that appears to float to the second level. **above left** A teak bar at the end of the living room pays homage to vintage cruising vessels. The owner's collection of model boat hulls hangs above it. **above** The dining room takes on a more formal tone. Pale blue walls are trimmed in white, highlighting the architecture of the space. **left** Pale yellow walls soften the home's whiteness while complementing the handsome Empire-style consoles and a collection of maritime paintings in the upstairs landing. **following pages** The protected veranda was designed to extend the living space to the outdoors.

island
attitudes

private paradise

Located in the heart of the French West Indies, St. Barthélemy, with its alluring style and distinctively French flavor, has become *the* winter destination of choice for discerning world travelers. International movie stars and celebrities in the art and fashion world are particularly attracted because complete seclusion is easily attainable.

Some of the most desirable villas can be rented through OVERSEAS CONNECTION including the starkly modern Villa La Dine II. Overlooking the entire Baie Ou Colombier, it has unobstructed views of St. Martin, Anguilla, and Saba. This resort home, set 700 feet up one of St. Barth's highest mountains, was designed by acclaimed architect STEVEN TICE for clients from the Northeast who regularly entertain friends and family. The layout incorporates three separate pavilions that accommodate six people. Each unit, with French doors that open to private verandas and the pool, is interconnected by terraces on the angled site, cleverly employing the slope of the hill and ocean vistas. Lush gardens follow the hilly terrain.

Tice's challenge was to create a structure harmonious with its setting and impervious to hurricanes, prevailing winds, and intense sunlight. His choice of the most basic

materials—concrete, zinc, and limestone—are used without artifice as distinctive architectural elements. Villa La Dine II not only fulfills its environmental requirements, it is contemporary design at its best—both restrained and distinctive.

photographer: PHILIPPE HOCHART FOR OVERSEAS CONNECTION, INC.
design budget: NOT DISCLOSED
square feet/meters: 10,000/929

center The front of the house showcases simple unadorned concrete sleeping pavilions capped by zinc gabled roofs. Limestone is used for floors, indoors and out, for a seamless effect. To create a bolder statement for the entry, Tice set indigenous stones into concrete for a graveled look. **above** The view from the pool overlooks Baie Ou Colombier as well as the panoramic vista of St. Martin, Anguilla, and Saba. Two different limestones were selected to form a herringbone pattern around the pool. **left** Cool, creamy limestone is used to offset the turquoise Caribbean water as well as the pool. It is virtually maintenance free.

opposite The clean and modern dining room can be opened on three sides to the outdoors for cross ventilation and to maximize views. **above left & above** Custom wood cabinetry, and a large sandblasted glass table and chairs from Knoll International keep the dining area spare but elegant. Gray limestone surrounded by a colored border outlines the eating area. No need for rugs in the tropics! **left** The interior concrete walls are painted cool, tropical colors. Simple Italian wicker couches, glass tables, and focused halogen lighting complete a clean, modernist look.

time and place

For Joan Gray of GRAYSON INTERIOR DESIGN, it was love at first sight. The moment this Connecticut designer and her husband crossed a narrow wooden bridge onto the tiny island, they felt they had stepped into another time and place. They knew this salty, crumbling house on Long Island Sound, marked for demolition, could be transformed into a personal expression of timeless design. And so began a tale of loving renovation, one that brought a turn-of-the-century Arts and Crafts-style home to the brink of the new millennium.

Years of neglect had left nearly every square inch of house, swimming pool, and grounds in need of restoration and re-design. The mossy stone and stucco exterior required sandblasting. Interiors were reconfigured to allow for a casual flow of space. New windows, artfully created to replicate the originals, were added to provide abundant light and glorious views of neighboring islands and Long Island Sound. Timeworn shag carpeting was removed and wood floors were stripped and refinished. Everything was to look authentic, as if it had been there forever.

Brick and mortar were just the beginning. To bring a contemporary spirit to a decades-old interior space, the designer applied her trademark creative touch—the color

white. Throughout the house white is used as a brilliant foil to highlight the eclectic collection of rustic and delicate treasures. Today, although still a work in progress, this house is all grown-up, but it proudly maintains a spirited attitude that will surely withstand the test of time.

photographer: ALEC HEMER
design budget: NOT DISCLOSED
square feet/meters: 5,000/464

center The original pool was demolished and a new one built, complete with twin gazebos used for storage, changing, or simply to support a rope hammock for an afternoon snooze. **above** In the living room shelves were built to showcase the couple's treasured collections. Kilim rugs and antique tapestry pillows layer color and texture over the creamy white palette. Window treatments are nothing more than wisps of exterior climbing ivy. **left** The stone, stucco, and shingle Arts and Crafts-style house overlooks Long Island Sound.

opposite Gray chose summery white duck to slipcover the living room furniture. A primitive zebra rug appears through a French glass coffee table. Poised on top are the designer's heirloom crystal decanters. **above** A center island defines the space of the large kitchen. A wall of windows in the breakfast area was added to provide light and greater views. **far left** Double French doors open to reveal the dining room. Skirted white slipcovered chairs surround a stately mahogany dining table bought at auction. **left** A cozy nook in the master bedroom boasts one of the best views in the house.

'50s refinement

Fisher Island, Florida
Waterside Homes
1998

What could better immortalize the golden age of Miami Beach than a decor that reflects the intense colors of white sand, blue-green water, and green sea grass? Annick Presles and Sophie-Eve Hocquard of LA MAISON FLEURIE were determined to add these unexpected jolts of color to a previously pale setting. They began re-designing a two-bedroom Fisher Island Mediterranean-style villa constructed by SANDY & BABCOCK for a savvy young international couple. The result is an upbeat and casual beach house, deeply saturated with the vibrant tones of its natural environment.

Bound by the brilliant blue waters of Biscayne Bay and the Atlantic Ocean, Fisher Island is just south of Miami Beach, yet it seems like worlds apart. The designers' goal for the project was to draw upon the ambience of this island community by reinterpreting the sharp contrast of its coastal colors. To maintain the level of refinement the clients desired, Presles and Hocquard incorporated richly polished cherry and walnut furniture to balance the textures and colors of fabric and glass. They tirelessly combed antique stores throughout southern Florida searching for funky, yet tasteful, fifties' accessories that were reminiscent of Miami's colorful heritage.

photographer: ROBERT BRANTLEY
design budget: NOT DISCLOSED
square feet/meters: 1,638/152

~~~~~~

center With terraces that face the beach, the house reinterprets a Mediterranean-style villa. **above** Saturated colors of grass and water are repeated in the ethnic upholstery pattern. **left** Terra-cotta tiles blend with the natural environment on the bayside patio.

opposite Interior and exterior blend in the living area. Metal and rattan "snail" chairs were discovered in a local antique shop. **left** Piped white slipcovers protect the sofas from an occasional wet swimsuit. Woven cotton rugs were chosen to be soft on bare feet. **below left** Louvered doors and shutters in the master bedroom suite provide access to sea breezes and the view. **below right** Sea green colored headboards and a fifties-style lamp add a whimsical touch to this bedroom.

goin' hunting

Whenever schedules and seasons permit, the New York owners of this rustic South Carolina hunting lodge enjoy an active vacation of hunting ducks, fishing, shrimping and crabbing. Their sprawling house, created by R. Christian Schmitt of SCHMITT SAMPSON ARCHITECTS and Thorndyke Williams of THORNDYKE WILLIAMS INTERIORS, is situated on an unusual circular site deep within the secluded woods of Bray's Island, a recently developed community carved out of a former 6,000-acre plantation.

In keeping with South Carolina's low country style, the architects configured the home around four hand-picked pine tree poles. Natural timber is used for the exposed double height ceiling which crowns a large great room typical of traditional Southern hunting lodges. All other rooms connect to this central core, which capitalizes on peaceful views of river life and marshlands.

Vertical glass doors which open onto wide shaded trellised terraces, and numerous electronically controlled clerestory windows, offer breezy cross ventilation. Because it was important to the naturalist owners to have their home blend with its marshland environment, the house was painted in the colors of the great outdoors. Ebony and deep browns

reflect aged wood; light green trim plays off the grassy marsh. The red roof refers to old restored Southern farmhouses, when shingles were often replaced with metal roofs and painted red. The result is an overall design that creates the sense of a family hunting lodge which has existed in these backwoods for generations.

photographer: © RION C. RIZZO/CREATIVE SOURCES PHOTOGRAPHY
design budget: $450,000
square feet/meters: 3,600/334

center Schmitt designed this hunting lodge in traditional low country rural vernacular style. It is situated on one circular acre on Bray's Island, a community developed from a 6,000-acre rice plantation. **above & left** A sweeping porch encircles the main house and its guest cottage. Outfitted with the obligatory Southern rocking chairs, it is the ideal place to quietly sip lemonade and take in the scenery.

opposite & above left The great room, which displays an open vaulted ceiling, serves as the main living space, dining area and kitchen. A wide loft, housing both office and extra sleeping quarters, is made of natural timber. **above** Thorndyke Williams was hired to design unpretentious and comfortable interiors. For the open kitchen he chose dark green walls, a perfect backdrop for the polished wood table, chairs and cabinets. **left** Comfortable wicker chairs in bold geometric patterns relate to the Indian wall-hanging placed over the fireplace. The custom rug displays a twig-patterned border.

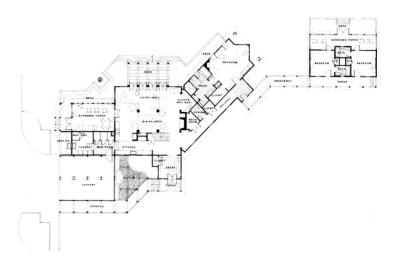

local color

Not far from São Paulo lies the charming, old native fishing island of Ilhabela, a beach resort of 15,000 inhabitants and center of championship sailing races. Here, a young urban family with three adolescent children who love water sports decided to build their weekend retreat.

The design for the home was entrusted to São Paulo architect Fernanda Ciampaglia of DIM ARQUITETOS ASSOCIADOS and was completed and overseen by the owner, a building construction manager. The overall feel of the house was intended to conform with the simplicity of the island's old fishing cottages, yet project a contemporary image in keeping with the young family's life style. Metal and glass generate luminosity and lightness, while the use of wood, brick and tile is reminiscent of fishermen's houses. Yellow, blue and green boat colors are counterbalanced with "white" floors composed of cement and sand.

The steep location—130 feet above sea level—required the use of numerous pillars to support the multilevel structure. Terraces adjoin the living room and bedroom, admitting sea breezes indoors. The effect is a magnificent view throughout the home, in a restful environment which blends traditional with new.

photographer: TUCA REINÉS
design budget: $250,000
square feet/meters: 3,100/288

center Large local stones are used for the steep front steps and the wall surrounding the pool.
above & left The sloping site seen from the balcony above the simply furnished living room shows the various levels of this unique property. Large floor to ceiling folding glass doors enable the living room to extend outdoors during the warm months.

opposite Architect Fernanda Ciampaglia designed the house to blend with the simple island architecture seen in old fishermen's cottages. The blue/green shutters echo the colors of the fishing boats. **above left** Living spaces conform to the sloping hill, as evident in the view from living room into the raised kitchen. **above** Glass and metal create a streamlined style, also allowing for luminous interiors. **left** The clean lined kitchen, like all other rooms, uses the colors of local fishing boats—ochre, yellow, blue and green. Glass fronted storage closets lend a decidedly modern touch.

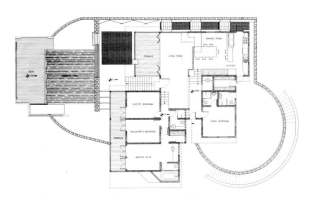

form & function

Historic Edgartown on scenic Martha's Vineyard is the quintessential New England harborside town. Having visited the island often, the client knew exactly what he wanted: a comfortable and informal, light-filled house with a glorious view of the harbor. A central location was required as he recently started using a wheelchair. His dream spot was found, but the house was in a sorry state.

Enlisting the help of architect Les Brown of STIRLING BROWN and interior designer Elizabeth Klee Speert of ELIZABETH SPEERT, the old structure was demolished down to the footprint. They constructed a casual, colorful home dictated by the mandate of attractive barrier-free design. Here the owner could maneuver his wheelchair under a sink, easily glide through a wider than normal door threshold, or lower himself onto the bed with minimum hardship. The architect's and designer's greatest achievement was their successful balance of form and function.

The warm, inviting home they designed provides few clues to the owner's strong personal requirements. A wheelchair lift was hidden behind attractive doors and sinks, and countertops and mirrors were placed at a lowered, more practical height. Additionally, ramps were installed from the

garden to the kitchen door. Carpets were tacked down, and even coffee tables and ottomans were given wheels so they could be pushed easily out of the way. Colorful and designed for comfort, this house is the ultimate user-friendly design.

photographer: ERIC ROTH, BOSTON MA
design budget: NOT DISCLOSED
square feet/meters: 3,500/325

center The Victorian shingle-style residence stands on a cliff above the Edgartown harbor. A smooth brick ramp/path leads from the house to town and ensures easy wheelchair access for the owner. **above** Designer Elizabeth Klee Speert put casters on the plump furniture to allow for easy movement, and chose a charming flat weave carpet which could withstand wheelchair tread. **left** An antique ship ornament of a naval officer brings a sense of whimsy to the foyer.

above Speert designed the furniture with a nautical circular motif inspired from the steering wheel of a sailboat. **above right** The architect installed a set of clerestory windows high above the stairwell and placed window frames inset with mirrors to maximize natural light. A painted sky ceiling mural intensifies the bright, outdoor feeling. **right & far right** In the kitchen, the countertops are lower and the toe kicks higher for easy maneuverability. **opposite** The Spanish bed, which rises lower from the floor than American made beds, also has circular carvings. The room's summery feel is created by Speert's use of flower strewn wallpaper and sheer drapery.

guest expectations

On Little Chimney Island there is always room for guests to stay for the night or take shelter from a storm. This is because Darrel Rippeteau of RIPPETEAU ARCHITECTS, designed a shingle-style cabin, reachable only by small boat, Jet Ski, or windsurfer, to accommodate plenty of overnight guests—even unexpected ones.

The Thousand Islands region, between New York State and Ontario, Canada, is made up of 1,900 tree-shaded granite islands ranging in size from a few square feet to many square miles. A professional couple chose Little Chimney Island for a family summer home located in the midst of a beautiful group of islands, yet completely private and surrounded by the deep clear waters of the St. Lawrence River.

The owners requested a design with ample living and sleeping space that reflected the style of older island residences. With Rippeteau, they toured the other islands culling examples of details and elements. Using local materials, they chose wood framing, cedar shingles, and granite for the rustic exterior. For the interiors, wood floors, trim, railings, and exposed framework lend an old-fashioned coziness to the camp-like setting. The result is a home that blends seamlessly with its environment.

photographer: HARLAN HAMBRIGHT © HAMBRIGHT ASSOC., INC.
design budget: NOT DISCLOSED
square feet/meters: 1,932/179

center The steep sloping roofs of St. Lawrence River houses are built to withstand snowy winters. Local granite was used for the chimney. **above** A gracefully curved porch is a lovely place to watch a summer sunrise. Enclosed by screens, it allows in only the gentle island breezes. **left** Reachable only by boat, Little Chimney Island is surrounded by the deep waters of the St. Lawrence River. The site was chosen for its 360° views.

opposite Wood railings, trim, and details are fashioned in the style of older island residences. **above** The ground floor is an open plan to maximize the sense of space within the 26' by 28' dimensions of the old stone foundation. **left** Simple white wicker furniture fills the breezy porch, lending a timeless ambience to the home.

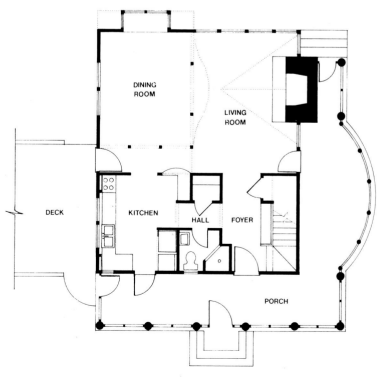

DINING ROOM

LIVING ROOM

DECK

KITCHEN

HALL

FOYER

PORCH

the far pavilions

While some people fantasize about living on a secluded tropical island, few actually buy the island and transform their dream into reality. A free-spirited New York couple did just that. They enlisted Drexel Patterson of ISLAND ARCHITECTS and interior design consultant Lawrence Peabody of PEABODY INTERNATIONAL to collaborate on the creation of a plantation-style paradise atop the tiny protrusion of volcanic rock called Little St. James. Lying just one-and-a-half miles from the southeastern tip of St. Thomas, the magnificent estate of Little St. James seems light years away from a modern Caribbean resort.

Glistening pavilions define the essence of island living. "The main goal was to make the house look as though it could have been on this island for a hundred years," the owner explained. Reminiscent of the Danish Colonial vernacular indigenous to the American Virgin Islands, it abounds with an architectural vocabulary that includes elliptical arches, shuttered and louvered French doors and openings, galleries and hip roofs without overhangs, and rubble stone walls. No glass or screen windows were used in the house. Instead, storm shutters fold back to capture warm tropical breezes and accent the 18-inch thick hurricane resistant cement walls.

photographer: © DON HEBERT PHOTOGRAPHY & JEAN PAGLIUSO PHOTOGRAPHY
design budget: NOT DISCLOSED
square feet/meters: 4,000/372

center above This tropical style home incorporates open arcades, lush courtyards, and numerous private terraces. Pyramid shaped roofs sparkle in the Caribbean sun. **center below** Dining al fresco provides a view of nearby St. Thomas. The brilliant tones of the sky and ocean are repeated in the gleaming tabletop. **above** A large pool overlooks the sea. It wraps around the base of an outcropping of natural rock and lush flora, conveniently screening the pool from prevailing winds. **left** Pipes hidden within the Ionic columns direct rainwater into underground cisterns used for irrigation.

opposite The casually elegant great room sets a stage for picture-perfect views framed by eleven identical doors. An exposed rafter and truss roofing system is both functional and decorative. **above** Mahogany sleigh beds and colorful furnishings lend intimacy to the children's pavilion. **left** Louvered doors and shutters allow the master bathroom suite access to breezes and the view. Interior coral stone veneers, indigenous to the location, are used throughout the pavilions of Little St. James.

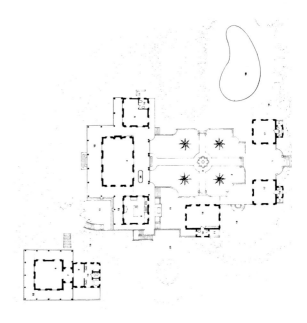

island lookout

Robert Hull and Craig Curtis of MILLER/HULL PARTNERSHIP, reinvented the tree house when they designed this rustic getaway on a steeply sloping site above Puget Sound. The owners wanted a house that was small and simple. Hull and Curtis complied by providing them with a 13-foot wide plan reminiscent of a forest service lookout station.

The rustic two-story house sits on a rocky cliff ending abruptly at the water's edge. Windows surround all four sides of the upper floor, which houses the living and dining areas, and the kitchen. Downstairs, the bedroom level is a solid structure with "punched" windows located by the built-in beds. Referring to influences of Scandinavian and Japanese inns, the architects used exposed timber and wood framing for the interiors.

Finding an unspoiled place and maintaining its natural state was no small feat for the owners and their innovative architects. Since there are virtually no cars or trucks allowed in this community of Decatur Island, building materials had to be brought in by barge and hand carried to the site. As a result, structural materials were kept short and light. When long spans were required, composite beams were bolted together and connected with exposed details.

Decatur Island, Washington
Waterside Homes
1998

photographer: MICHAEL SHOPENN PHOTOGRAPHY
design budget: $100,000
square feet/meters: 840/78

center With unobstructed views of Puget Sound, the two-story structure contrasts a solid base with an upper floor of timber and glass. The house is entered from a bridge to the upper floor. above Sunshine floods the room, highlighting the built-in furniture in the living/dining area. The cabin is effciently heated by a wood burning stove. left Even the kitchen has windows on the world, with clear views of Puget Sound.

virgin territory

Surrounded by a coral reef and some of the finest cruising waters in the Caribbean, Necker Island had little more than neckerberry bushes and some grazing goats when British entrepreneur Richard Branson first flew over it. Branson bought this British Virgin Island and hired John Osman of OSMAN, ADAMS & PARTNERS ARCHITECTS and Lory Johansson and June Scott of ERGO DESIGN WORKS to create a house that would enhance its natural beauty and maintain the owner's feeling of being a castaway in a tropical paradise. For the main house, Osman walked Necker's 74 acres and selected the site of "Devil's Hill," which took six months to blast. He designed a structure to follow its profile, with the roof replacing the hill's peak.

The tropical climate and proclivity to hurricane conditions dictated deep foundations and posts, and wide overhangs. Many building materials had to be imported—stone from England and hardwood beams from Brazil. Since Branson was intrigued by the culture and crafts of Bali, he decided to merge the design influences of one island with the other, the result being a decidedly Caribbean home with an exotic Indonesian spirit.

Island Attitudes

To achieve the airy Balinese style, the designers spent three months in Bali buying antique Dutch colonial furnishings and handcrafted carvings. Balinese teak, which stands up to the humid, salty air of the West Indies, was selected for most of the furniture. White-on-white embroideries and vibrant batiks and ikats, used as pillows and throws give the rooms a contemporary feel.

photographer: DOUGAL D. THORNTON ASSOCIATES
design budget: NOT DISCLOSED
square feet/meters: 16,000/1,486

center above The main house, its two pavilions separated by a breezeway, has roofs with deep overhangs. center below Stone tile from Yorkshire, England surrounds the pool, which seems to disappear into the Caribbean. above & left Breezy dining terraces amidst tropical growth are set upon the hill site, where the artful element of Balinese sculpture highlights the spectacular view.

above The light-filled great room welcomes relaxation and quiet recreation. Oversized bamboo chairs and teak settees are piled high with colorful batik pillows from Bali.
right Each guest bedroom has a spectacular view of the sparkling water and neighboring islands. The designers used bold textiles to highlight the delicate white embroidered bedcovering.

left The romantic four-poster bed in the master bedroom has Dutch colonial posts, a foot-board from a Balinese opium bed, and a head-board from an antique bench— all assembled by local craftspeople. below left A whirl-pool is accented by Balinese arti-facts. below All of the construction, including this tennis court, follows the contours of the hill.

simple
pleasures

collector's cottage

A few years ago, consummate interior designer Jack Phillips of JACK PHILLIPS DESIGN extended the versatility of his talents when he moved into a small cottage outside of Vero Beach, Florida.

The 2,000-square-foot home, shaded by the leaves of a stately oak tree, was one of a number of cozy residences built in the mid-seventies in a tiny seaside enclave called "Summer Place." The dwelling had the no fuss, simple beach cottage look the designer had often dreamed about owning, and he preserved the comfortably inviting exterior. A path of white pebbles leads visitors to the trim, weathered blue/gray cottage, its windows ornamented by fresh white shutters. The garden blooms year-round in a profusion of flowering plants. Hanging on a massive branch from Phillips' beloved oak tree is a three-tiered birdhouse full of delightful chirping sounds. Under it rests a white bent-willow bench. Once inside the front door, guests are treated to a panoply of visual delights. Although a master stylist for many a Mediterranean mansion, the designer wanted his own home to reflect a simple cottage vernacular. Indeed it does. It not only reflects his warm personality, but also his pleasure in collecting— everything from creamware, to baskets, to nauticalia.

photographer: ROBERT BRANTLEY
design budget: $100,000
square feet/meters: 2,000/186

center The stately 100-year-old oak tree was what drew Fhillips to the house when it was built 22 years ago. The simple, unobtrusive cottage exterior blends in quietly in this tiny community called "Summer Place". **above** The den is swathed in chambray fabric and furnished with white wicker for a carefree year-round summer look. A mahogany butler's tray serves as a coffee table. **left** The community dock leads to the beach at the tiny enclave Fhillips calls home.

opposite Phillips' clients have nicknamed him, the "100% cotton man." In his own living room, a comfortable mix of deep sofas and large upholstered chairs, he maintains the same standard—only 100% cottons! **above** The designer juxtaposes objects and materials, such as antique boxes, pitchers, hurricane lamps, and nautical inspired pillows to create still-life vignettes which are attractive as well as useful. **right** The informal dining room is furnished with a sturdy oak table. Rich wood also composes the rustic beamed ceiling. **below** A new, whimsical wrought-iron bed takes center stage in the lively nautically inspired guest room. A valence for the blue and white striped drapes looks like it came from a sailboat. The quilt is early American.

into the woods

When a couple who enjoyed fishing, hunting and boating with their three grown children wanted to unwind during long weekends and holidays, they purchased several acres of land in a rural community in the South Carolina low country. The site, although only 20 miles from Beaufort, was located down a long dirt road with a dramatic marshland view of the Chechessee river.

The owners desired a family compound, comprised of a series of structures strong enough to withstand severe hurricanes with only minimal maintenance since the home would be used seasonally. Offering generous artistic freedom, they turned to renowned R. Christian Schmitt of SCHMITT SAMPSON ARCHITECTS and Thorndyke Williams of THORNDYKE WILLIAMS INTERIOR DESIGN.

The project evolved into a cluster of three low-key buildings styled in the rural vernacular which blend easily into the woods and marshland area. The main house is designed around a large great room replete with dramatic timber vaulted ceilings, evoking the spirit of an old Carolina hunting lodge. Bedrooms, a screened porch, dining room, and large country kitchen are offshoots from the central axis and designed so that all principle living

spaces have views of the marshland and surrounding water. A two bedroom guest house and separate garage complete the family compound.

photographer: © RION C. RIZZO/CREATIVE SOURCES PHOTOGRAPHY, INC.
design budget: $1,500,000
square feet/meters: 7,000/650

center The family compound consists of a main house, guest cottage and garage. Deep shaded porches supported by sturdy columns are consistent with classic Southern design. **above** All rooms open onto a raised brick terrace. Each of the three buildings were built on slab over the terrace area, ensuring that the site would be high enough to withstand often heavy seasonal flooding. **left** The red metal roofs hark back to the local tradition of farmhouse renovation when old wooden shingles were replaced by metal and painted red.

previous pages Nestled in the rural landscape, the main house boasts high beamed ceilings, red metal roofs, a large square living room window and high clerestory fenestration. **opposite** Revealing its skeletal structure, the home's unsheathed timber beams are laid out in a rural design in keeping with the low country genre. **above left & above** The home's open loft-like design allows for free airflow and natural cooling. Simple, rustic American furniture and decorative arts, as well as cotton covered upholstered pieces create an elegant and comfortably livable seasonal home. **left** Rich wood cabinets and shelving complement the warmth of the fireplace in this reading corner.

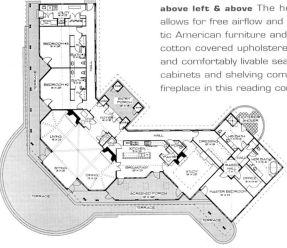

primitive instincts

Fleixeiras Beach, on the northeastern coast of Brazil, is known as the "land of light". Its beauty is defined by brilliant sunlight reflecting off white dunes and palm trees that bend to ocean breezes. When GERSON CASTELO BRANCO was asked to design a weekend house in this spectacular location for a couple and their four children, he immediately envisioned a "Paraqueiras Brasileira," a structure in the vernacular style of the local fishing villages. Its wooden construction, dune-col_____ rick sides and carnauba palm roof naturally enhar___ magnificent scenery of this beach resort. It is at on__ contemporary and compatible with the indigenous architectural heritage of the region.

The owners wanted a large home with an open plan that could harness the frequent strong winds that provide necessary ventilation. The main floor contains a dining room, kitchen and bar—all with access to outdoor terraces for viewing the magnificent sunsets. Six large bedrooms, on the ground floor and upstairs, host the family and weekend guests.

To give the house its primitive appearance, the entire structure was built with carnauba—frames, pillars, beams and roof timbers. ALBERTO PINHO decorated the

Fleixeiras, Ceará, Brazil
Waterside Homes
1998

interiors to complement the naturalist architecture. He used carnauba trunks as well for sofas, tables, and beds, and upholstered them in natural fibers. "Everything is very simple, a reminder of Brazil's cultural background, and promotes the art of good living," said Gerson.

photographer: JOAŌ RIBEIRO
design budget: $350,000
square feet/meters: 8,074/750

center The "paraqueira" is compatible with its environment—the color of bricks derived from a tinted mixture of glue and sand. **above** The design concept is to eliminate the boundary between interior and exterior; the shaded veranda integrates with the beach and beyond. **left** Sunny terraces provide comfortable places to rest. Pinho placed bold colored cushions on the custom carnauba settees.

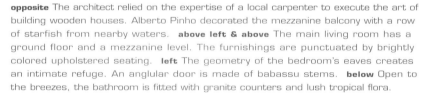

opposite The architect relied on the expertise of a local carpenter to execute the art of building wooden houses. Alberto Pinho decorated the mezzanine balcony with a row of starfish from nearby waters. **above left & above** The main living room has a ground floor and a mezzanine level. The furnishings are punctuated by brightly colored upholstered seating. **left** The geometry of the bedroom's eaves creates an intimate refuge. An anglular door is made of babassu stems. **below** Open to the breezes, the bathroom is fitted with granite counters and lush tropical flora.

maine attraction

For more than three generations, a family from Washington, D.C. has summered in a simple cabin in the woodlands of western Maine. The current owners, anticipating their retirement years, decided the easy, unpretentious Maine life style would suit their needs. They knew their beloved family cabin needed major transformation to become a full-time home. Maryland architect Mark McInturff of MCINTURFF ARCHITECTS, who is known for incorporating local vernacular design and indigenous materials into his modernist style, was their confident choice. The residence he created after knocking down the old cabin was inspired by the Adirondack "camp" compounds of the late 19th century.

The clients requested that all principle living spaces be situated on one floor for easy access. Primary concern was given to maximizing views of the pond which is active with wildlife in every season. McInturff designed a 3,000-square-foot home using local maple and fir. His spatial layout encompassed three connecting gabled spaces in progressively smaller sizes. The architectural configuration is reminiscent of local connected house and barn compounds. The largest space houses the living room, dining area and kitchen and looks out to the pond. The second space is set

Simple Pleasures

aside for the master bedroom and a screened porch, with guest bedrooms on the second floor. While the three gabled components of the residence are lit by cupolas similar to those seen in local barns, McInturff set a contemporary tone with an open floor plan and clean lined architecture.

photographer: JULIA HEINE/McINTURFF ARCHITECTS
design budget: NOT DISCLOSED
square feet/meters: 2,400/223

center above McInturff is well known for his use of indigenous materials. Local fieldstones are employed for front steps and structural support. **center below** The dining area furniture is all Stickley. The simple, clean lines of a Shaker rocking chair and maple cabinet warm the living room. **above** Natural maple wood used for beams and rafters are left exposed to underscore the clean, contemporary architecture. **left** McInturff's architecture blends harmoniously with its natural wooded environment. Large picture windows focus on the active water view.

opposite Holding court in the living room is the massive fireplace crafted from local fieldstone and bluestone. The grided windows flanking the fireplace admit natural light into the master bedroom (housed in the second connecting gabled space). **above** Two tree trunks, bought from a local toy manufacturer, are used as supporting columns for the living room. McInturff used Shaker and Stickley furniture in the dining area. **above right** The connecting rafters take their cue from local house and barn assemblages. **right** Large double height windows look out toward the pond and flood the rooms with light.

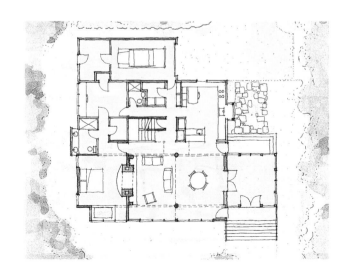

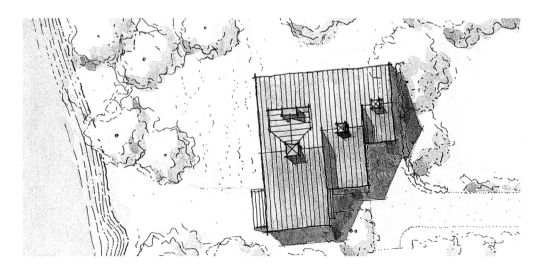

coming about

These days the word "retirement" can have many meanings. For one seaside loving couple with a passion for sailing, retirement meant a new Florida home with immediate access to the boat they built themselves. Their frequent sailing excursions made it necessary to have a home with ease of maintenance, which they could close up and leave whenever the gulf waters beckoned.

Few appreciate the forces of weather better than sailors. So when they chose architect and designer Suzanne Martinson of SUZANNE MARTINSON ARCHITECTS to design their home at Punta Gorda Isles, the couple knew she would find elegant and functional solutions to the demands of southwest Florida's climate. Martinson used a "dog trot" construction with a hip roof, and made the house hurricane-resistant through reinforced concrete block with poured continuous footing below grade. Since Punta Gorda is often plagued with drought and water rationing, the design of the house incorporated a 14,000 gallon cistern formed by displacing a piece from the lower level. The top surface of the cistern became the exterior rear terrace.

To take full advantage of the breezes, the main living space was located on the second level. The living room, kitchen,

and master bedroom gain maximal views of the protected estuary. Throughout the home, classic modern furnishings, white walls, and terra-cotta floors underscore a modernist feeling of uncluttered comfort.

photographer: © STEVEN BROOKE STUDIOS
design budget: $100,000
square feet/meters: 2,400/223

center Architecturally, the house is organized in layers, oriented to the southern water view. **above** A commanding outdoor masonry stairway dramatically focuses on the clean symmetry of the home. **left** The home affords immediate access to the dock, where the clients' catamaran waits.

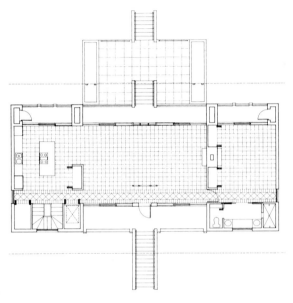

previous pages When the glass doors are open, the house takes on a pavilion-like quality. The remaining screens allow for ample ventilation. **opposite** The windows and doors are framed in black to contrast the white envelope of the house. The screen was designed by Suzanne Martinson. **left** The second-story living space is continuous, open, and modernist in concept. **below** The classic modern ash chair offsets the bold stripings on the bed.

summer whites

Panorama is a word that seems to have been invented for places like eastern Long Island. Cliffside homes, ocean beaches, and endless views of the Atlantic coexist with a rich heritage of farms and fishing. Thirteen years ago Vicente Wolf of VICENTE WOLF ASSOCIATES and his then partner, Bob Patino, selected a seemingly ordinary seventies suburban-style house with its principle asset—an amazing view. Wolf, using his signature color white, lovingly transformed this house of dark paneled walls and dated carpets into an enlightened oasis of meditative calm.

First, he tackled the interior structure—the entryway was changed, rooms were gutted, and the entire layout was reconfigured. He removed insignificant windows and some of their surrounding walls from the original structure, allowing the ocean facing boundaries to disappear into the expansive view beyond. Creating a carefree retreat for himself and weekend guests, Wolf included extra bedrooms, a large kitchen geared to informal entertaining, and plenty of comfortable seating indoors and out.

In contrast to the inspired design of the bleached white interior, most of the gray sided exterior was left intact. Wolf focused on the landscape, which incorporates gardens,

decks, and a stunning pool overlooking the beach. By integrating the outdoor and indoor space, he created a serene, yet inviting extension of the space within.

photographer: VICENTE WOLF
design budget: NOT DISCLOSED
square feet/meters: 5,000/465

center Captain's chairs cloaked in white canvas form a relaxing conversation corner overlooking the beach. **above** A dramatic swimming pool crowns the site above the beach and ocean. **left** Crisp white fabrics used for slipcovers and upholstery maintain a year-round summer mood. The milk-painted table is one of Wolf's yard sale finds.

opposite When not designing interiors, Wolf focuses on his other passion—photography. Intriguing images line the living room banquette. **above left** A glimpse into the kitchen exposes open shelving and a glass door refrigerator. **above** A white Formica pedestal dining table is surrounded by chairs slipcovered in Belgian linen. **left** The master bathroom boasts a 19-century French copper bathtub and a table of Wolf's design. Doors slide open to a wooded deck.

directory

ARCHITECTS & DESIGNERS

Bierly-Drake Associates, Inc.
Lee Bierly
Christopher Drake
17 Arlington Street
Boston, Massachusetts 02116
Tel: (617) 247-0081
Fax: (617) 247-6395

Gerson Castelo Branco
Monsenhor Bruno 750
Fortaleza, Ceará
Brazil
Tel: (55) 85-264-2165
Fax: (55) 85-261-4146

Danadjieva & Koenig Associates
Angela Danadjieva
P.O. Box 939
Tiburon, California 94920
Tel: (415) 435-2000
Fax: (415) 435-0896

Design Connection
Jean-Pierre Heim
Galal Mahmoud
24 Rue Vieille du Temple
Paris 75004
France
Tel: (33) 1-48-870708
Fax: (33) 1-42-770181

DIM Arquitetos Associados
Fernanda Ciampaglia
Rua da Consolação 3741
São Paulo, São Paulo
Brazil
Tel/Fax: (55) 11-306-11716

Elizabeth Speert Inc.
Elizabeth Klee Speert
53 Barnard Avenue
Watertown, Massachusetts 02172
Tel: (617) 926-3725
Fax: (617) 926-3376

Ergo Design Works
Lory Johansson
June Scott, ASID
8112 1/2 West 3rd Street D
Los Angeles, California
Tel: (213) 658-8901
Fax: (213) 658-8903

Geoffrey Bradfield, Inc.
Geoffrey N. Bradfield
105 East 63rd Street
New York, New York 10021
Tel: (212) 758-1773
Fax: (212) 688-1751

Gozzo Estate Homes
Gregory Gozzo
9121 North Military Trail
Palm Beach Gardens, Florida 33410
Tel: (561) 626-8062
Fax: (561) 832-2360

Grayson Interior Design
Joan Gray
1248 Post Road East
Westport, Connecticut 06880
Tel: (203) 222-7661
Fax: (203) 221-8263

Gwathmey Siegel & Associates Architects
Charles Gwathmey
475 Tenth Avenue
New York, New York 10018
Tel: (212) 947-1240
Fax: (212) 967-0890

Island Architects
Drexel Patterson
7632 Herschel Avenue
La Jolla, California 92037
Tel: (619) 459-9291
Fax: (619) 456-0351

Jack Fhillips Interior Design
Jack Fhillips
7 Via Parigi
Palm Beach, Florida 33480
Tel: (561) 659-4459
Fax: (561) 659-0949

Jackson Poole Rabinowitz PTY Ltd.
Mark Jackson
Dennis Rabinowitz
239 Pacific Highway
North Sydney, New South Wales 2071
Australia
Tel: (61) 29-966-1133
Fax: (61) 29-966-1323

John Chan Design Ltd.
John Chan
34 Wyndham Street
Hong Kong
China
Tel: (852) 252-10050
Fax: (852) 252-67425

La Maison Fleurie, Inc.
Annick Presles
Sophie-Eve Hocquard
139 North County Road
Palm Beach, Florida 33480
Tel: (561) 833-1083
Fax: (561) 833-9318

Legorreta Arquitectos
Ricardo Legorreta
Palacio de Versalles
285-A Lomas Reforma
Mexico City 11020
Mexico D.F.
Tel: (52) 5-251-9698
Fax: (52) 5-596-6162

McInturff Architects
Mark McInturff
4220 Leeward Place
Bethesda, Maryland 20816
Tel: (301) 229-3705
Fax: (301) 229-6380

McWhorter Architects
Carey McWhorter
30 Gardenia Street
Seagrove Beach, Florida 32459
Tel: (904) 231-1750
Fax: (904) 231-1735

The Miller/Hull Partnership
Robert Hull, FAIA
Craig Curtis, AIA
911 Western Avenue
Seattle, Washington 98104
Tel: (206) 682-6837
Fax: (206) 682-5692

Mitchell J. Rubin Associates, Inc.
Mitchell J. Rubin
881 Seventh Avenue
New York, New York 10019
Tel: (212) 765-0801
Fax: (212) 765-0890

Osman, Adams & Partners, Architects
John Osman
P.O. Box 833
Road Town, Tortola
British Virgin Islands
Tel: (809) 494-2343
Fax: (809) 494-5956

Payette Associates, Inc.
Thomas M. Payette, FAIA, RIBA
285 Summer Street
Boston, Massachusetts 02210
Tel: (617) 342-8200
Fax: (617) 342-8202

Peabody International
Lawrence Peabody
7 Cutter Hill Road
Rindge, New Hampshire 03461
Tel: (603) 899-3334
Fax: (603) 899-5228

Peter Pennoyer Architects, P.C.
Peter Pennoyer
Thomas Nugent
1239 Broadway
New York, New York 10001
Tel: (212) 779-9765
Fax: (212) 779-3814

Alberto Pinho
Avenida Zezé Diogo 5150
Fortaleza, Ceará
Brazil
Tel: (55) 85-252-2546
Fax: (55) 85-252-2653

Richard Mervis Design, Inc.
Richard Mervis
654 Madison Avenue
New York, New York 10021
Tel: (212) 371-6363
Fax: (212) 371-6396

Rippeteau Architects, P.C.
Darrel Rippeteau, AIA
1530 14th Street, NW
Washington, D.C. 20005
Tel: (202) 265-0777
Fax: (202) 483-0639

Robert Grubb & Associates PTY Ltd.
Robert Grubb
211 Bourke Street
East Sydney, New South Wales
Australia
Tel: (61) 29-360-1255
Fax: (61) 29-332-1199

Sandy & Babcock, Inc.
2727 SW 26th Avenue
Miami, Florida 33133
Tel: (305) 856-2021

Schmitt Sampson Architects
R. Christian Schmitt
12-A Vanderhorst Street
Charleston, South Carolina 29403
Tel: (803) 727-3140
Fax: (803) 727-3143

Sig Bergamin Interiors, Inc.
Sig Bergamin
20 East 69th Street
New York, New York 10021
Tel: (212) 327-4068
Fax: (212) 861-3667

Steven Ehrlich Architects
Steven Ehrlich, FAIA
Marlo Wolfe
2210 Colorado Avenue
Santa Monica, California 90404
Tel: (310) 828-6700
Fax: (310) 828-7710

Stirling Brown
Les Brown
One Mount Vernon Street
Winchester, Massachusetts 01890
Tel: (781) 721-1310

Studio Marco Aurelio Menegazzo
S/O Ltd.
Marco Aurelio Keller Menegazzo
Rua Conego Eugenio Leite
274-A Jardin América
São Paulo, São Paulo
Brazil
Tel: (55) 11-282-9745
Fax: (55) 11-282-2772

Suzanne Martinson Architects, Inc.
    Suzanne Martinson
7910 SW 54th Court
Miami, Florida 33032
Tel: (305) 667-3944
Fax: (305) 663-0405

Thorndyke Williams Interior Design
    Thorndyke Williams
P.O. Box 506
Beaufort, South Carolina 29901
Tel: (803) 524-7688

Vicente Wolf Associates
    Vicente Wolf
333 West 39th Street
New York, New York 10018
Tel: (212) 465-0590
Fax: (212) 465-0639

William Kite Architects, Inc.
    William L. Kite, Jr., AIA
One Meeting Street
Providence, Rhode Island 02903
Tel: (401) 272-0240
Fax: (401) 351-8985

PHOTOGRAPHERS

Aaron Usher III Photography
    Aaron Usher III
1080 Newport Avenue
Pawtucket, Rhode Island 02861
Tel/Fax: (401) 725-4595

Alec Hemer Photo
    Alec Hemer
81 Bedford Street
New York, New York 10014
Tel/Fax: (212) 924-7125

Assassi Productions
    Farshid Assassi
3221 Calle Rosales
Santa Barbara, California 93105
Tel: (805) 895-7703
Fax: (805) 682-2158

Patrick Bingham-Hall
85 Commonwealth Street
Surry Hills, New South Wales
Australia
Fax: (61) 29-281-0301

Brantley Photography
    Robert Brantley
    Carmel Brantley
1033 Brooks Lane
Delray Beach, Florida 33483
Tel/Fax: (561) 265-0995

Brian Vanden Brink Photographer
    Brian Vanden Brink
P.O. Box 419
Rockport, Maine 04856
Tel: (207) 236-4035
Fax: (207) 236-0704

Gary Clark
Southern Progress Corporation
2100 Lakeshore Road
Birmingham, Alabama 35209
Tel: (205) 877-5884
Fax: (205) 877-6990

Grey Crawford
1714 Lyndon Street
South Pasedena, California 91030
Tel: (213) 413-4299
Fax: (818) 441-3159

Creative Sources Photography, Inc.
    Rion C. Rizzo
6095 Lake Forest Drive
Atlanta, Georgia 30328
Tel: (404) 843-2141
Fax: (404) 250-1807

Don Hebert Photography
    Don Hebert
P.O. Box 11694
St. Thomas, U.S. Virgin Islands 00801
Tel/Fax: (809) 777-6484

Dougal D. Thornton Associates
    Dougal D. Thornton
P.O. Box 984
Road Town, Tortola
British Virgin Islands
Tel: (809) 494-4277
Fax: (809) 494-5801

Eric Roth Studio
    Eric Roth
337 Summer Street
Boston, Massachusetts 02210
Tel: (617) 338-5358
Fax: (617) 338-6098

Julia Heine
4220 Leeward Place
Bethesda, Maryland 20816
Tel: (501) 229-3705
Fax: (501) 229-6380

Housel Photo
    James F. Housel
80 Vine Street
Seattle, Washington 98121
Tel: (206) 441-5067
Fax: (206) 441-8831

Jean Pagliuso Photography
Jean Pagliuso
526 West 26th Street
New York, New York 10001
Tel: (212) 675-4299
Fax: (212) 675-4692

Lourdes Legorreta
Sierra Nevada 460
Lomas de Chapultepec
Mexico City
Mexico D.F.
Tel: (52) 5-520-0745
Fax: (52) 5-520-4045

Michael Shopenn Photography
Michael Shopenn
13826 SE 62nd Street
Bellevue, Washington 98006
Tel: (206) 283-5393

Overseas Connection, Inc.
Philippe Hochart
P.O. Box 1800
Long Wharf Promenade
Sag Harbor, New York 11963
Tel: (516) 725-9308
Fax: (516) 725-5825

Pascal Blancon Photography
Pascal Blancon
253 Matsonford Road
Radnor, Pennsylvania 19087
Tel: (610) 687-1090

Phillip H. Ennis Photography
Phillip H. Ennis
98 Smith Street
Freeport, New York 11520
Tel: (516) 379-4273
Fax: (516) 379-1126

Joaõ Ribeiro
Editora Açaõ Publicaçoes
Cel. Palimércio de Rezende
25 Butantã
São Paulo, Brazil
Tel: (55) 11-840-0346
Fax: (55) 14-263-2021

Sam Gray Photography
Sam Gray
23 Westwood Road
Wellesley, Massachusetts 02181
Tel: (617) 237-2711
Fax: (617) 482-1844

George Shelley
1522 SW 13th Court
Fort Lauderdale, Florida 33312
Tel: (305) 761-7706

Eric Sierins
4 Glen Street
Milsons Point, New South Wales
Australia
Tel/Fax: (61) 29-957-3166

Steven Brooke Studios
Steven Brooke
7910 SW 54th Court
Miami, Florida 33143
Tel: (305) 667-8075
Fax: (305) 663-0405

Tom Bonner Photography
1201 Abbot Kinney Boulevard
Venice, California 90291
Tel: (310) 396-7125
Fax: (310) 396-4792

Tuca Reinés Photo
Tuca Reinés
Rua Emanuel Kant 58
São Paulo, São Paulo 04536
Brazil
Tel: (55) 11-506-19127
Fax: (55) 11-852-8735

William C. Minarich Photography, Inc.
William C. Minarich
2280 Linwood Avenue
Naples, Florida 33962
Tel: (941) 774-2800
Fax: (941) 774-3900

Vicente Wolf
333 West 39th Street
New York, New York 10018
Tel: (212) 465-0590
Fax: (212) 465-0639

Wade Zimmerman
9 East 97th Street
New York, New York 10029
Tel: (212) 427-8784
Fax: (212) 427-3526

SPECIAL CONSULTANTS

New Hall's Wheels
P.O. Box 380784
Cambridge, Massachusetts 02238
Tel: (617) 628-0424

Overseas Connection, Inc.
Steven Tice
P.O. Box 1800
Long Wharf Promenade
Sag Harbor, New York 11963
Tel: (516) 725-9308
Fax: (516) 725-5825

index

ARCHITECTS & DESIGNERS

PHOTOGRAPHERS

SPECIAL CONSULTANTS

acknowledgments

We wish to offer our heartfelt thanks to all those who generously contributed to the completion of Waterside Homes.

This book would not have been possible without the dedicated assistance of our friends at PBC International. From conception to production, their enthusiasm and perseverance never waned.

A book such as this is truly a team effort. We are indebted to the following people:

To the architects and designers, who so generously contributed their completed works—and to the photographers who artfully brought these visions to life

To the owners of the magnificent waterside homes, who graciously allowed us to peek into their private worlds

To Katherine Pearson, Editor of Coastal Living, for her insightful foreword

To a special group of photographers, publicists, designers, and friends who helped connect us to many celebrated projects—Karen J. Downs of Coastal Living; Phillip Ennis; Joan Grey; Beverly and David Neufeld; New Hall's Wheels, Inc.; Overseas Connection, Inc.; Lucinda Schweikert; Mike Strohl; Vicente Wolf; Wade Zimmerman

To our families, for their love and support.

Marcie & Susan

Marcie Stuchin & Susan Abramson
Waterside Homes
PBC International, Inc.